MW01298237

Catholic Commentary on

Genesisi

BY:

GEORGE HAYDOCK

INTRODUCTION

The Hebrews now entitle all the Five Books of Moses, from the initial words, which originally were written like one continued word or verse; but the Septuagint have preferred to give the titles the most memorable occurrences of each work. On this occasion, the Creation of all things out of nothing strikes us with peculiar force. We find a refutation of all the heathenish mythology, and of the world's eternity, which Aristotle endeavored to establish. We behold the short reign of innocence, and the origin of sin and misery, the dispersion of nations, and the providence of God watching over his chosen people, till the death of Joseph, about the year of the world 2369 (Usher) 2399 (Salien and Tirinus), the year before Christ 1631. We shall witness the same care in the other Books of Scripture, and adore his wisdom and goodness in preserving to himself faithful witnesses, and a true Holy Catholic Church, in all ages, even when the greatest corruption seemed to overspread the land. (Haydock)

CHAPTER I
VERSE 1

Beginning. As St. Matthew begins his Gospel with the same title as this work, *the Book of the Generation,* or Genesis, so St. John adopts the first words of Moses, *in the beginning;* but he considers a much higher order of things, even the consubstantial Son of God, *the same with God* from all eternity, forming the universe, in the beginning of time, in conjunction with the other two Divine Persons, *by the word of his power; for all things were made by Him,* the Undivided Deity. (Haydock) --- *Elohim,* the *Judges* or Gods, denoting plurality, is joined with a verb singular, *he created,* whence many, after Peter Lombard, have inferred, that in this first verse of Genesis the adorable mystery of the Blessed Trinity is insinuated, as they also gather from various other passages of the Old Testament, though it was not clearly revealed till our Savior came himself to be the *finisher of our faith.*(Calmet) --- The Jews being a carnal people and prone to idolatry, might have been in danger of misapplying this great mystery, and therefore an explicit belief of it was not required of them in general. The word bara, *created,* is here determined by tradition and by reason to mean a production out of nothing, though it be used also to signify the forming of a thing out of pre-existing matter. (ver. 21, 27) (Calmet) --- The first cause of all things must be God, who, in a moment, spoke, and *heaven and earth* were made, heaven with all the Angels; and the whole mass of the elements, in a state of confusion, and blended together, out of which the beautiful order, which was afterwards so admirable, arose in the space of six days; thus God was pleased to manifest his free choice in opposition to those Pagans who attributed all to blind chance or fate. *Heaven* is here placed first, and is not declared *empty* and dark like the earth; that we may learn to raise our minds and hearts above this land of trial, to that our true country, where we may enjoy God for ever. (Haydock)

VERSE 2

Spirit of God, giving life, vigor, and motion to things, and preparing the waters for the sacred office of baptism, in which, by the institution of Jesus Christ, we must be born again; and, like spiritual *fishes,* swim amid the tempestuous billows of this world. (v. Tert.[Tertullian] &c) (Worthington) (Haydock)---This Spirit is what the Pagan philosophers styled the Soul of the World. (Calmet) --- If we compare their writings with the books of Moses and the prophets, we shall find that they agree in many points. (Haydock)

VERSE 3

Light. The sun was made on the fourth day, and placed in the firmament to distinguish the seasons, &c.; but the particles of fire were created on the first day, and by their, or the earth's motion, served to discriminate day from the preceding night, or *darkness,* which was *upon the face of the deep.* (Haydock) --- Perhaps this body of light might resemble the bright cloud which accompanied the Israelites, Exodus xiv. 19, or the three first days might have a kind of imperfect sun, or be like one of our cloudy days. Nothing can be defined with certainty respecting the nature of this primeval light. (Calmet)

VERSE 4

Good; beautiful and convenient: --- *he divided light* by giving it qualities incompatible with *darkness,* which is not anything substantial, and therefore Moses does not say it was created. (Calmet) --- While our hemisphere enjoys the day, the other half of the world is involved in darkness. St. Augustine supposes the fall and punishment of the apostate angels are here insinuated. (L. *imp. de Gen.*) (Haydock)

VERSE 6

A firmament. By this name is here understood the whole space between the earth and the highest stars. The lower part of which divideth the waters that are upon the earth, from those that are above in the clouds. (Challoner) --- The Hebrew *Rokia* is translated *stereoma,* solidity by the Septuagint and expansion by most of the moderns. The heavens are often represented as a tent spread out, Psalm ciii 3. (Calmet)

VERSE 7

Above the firmament and stars, according to some of the Fathers; or these waters were vapors and clouds arising from the earth, and really divided from the lower waters contained in the sea. (Calmet)

VERSE 11

Seed in itself, either in the fruit or leaves, or slips. (Menochius) --- At the creation, trees were covered with fruit in Armenia, while in the more northern regions they would not even have leaves: Calmet hence justly observes, that the question concerning the season of the year when the world began, must be understood only with reference to that climate in which Adam dwelt. Scaliger asserts, that the first day corresponds with our 26th of October, while others, particularly the Greeks, fix it upon the 25th of March, on which day Christ was conceived; and, as some Greeks say, was born and nailed to the cross. The great part of respectable authors declare for the vernal equinox, when the year is in all its youth and beauty. (Haydock) See Tirinus and Salien's Annals, the year before Christ 4053.

VERSE 14

For signs. Not to countenance the delusive observations of astrologers, but to give notice of rain, of the proper seasons for sowing, &c. (Menochius) --- If the sun was made on the first day, as some assert, there is nothing new created on this fourth day. By specifying the use and creation of these heavenly bodies, Moses shows the folly of the Gentiles, who adored them as gods, and the impiety of those who pretend that human affairs are under the fatal influence of the planets. The Hebrew term *mohadim,* which is here rendered *seasons,* may signify either *months,* or the *times for assembling* to worship God; (Calmet) a practice, no doubt, established from the beginning every week, and probably also the first day of the *new moon,* a day which the Jews afterwards religiously observed. Plato calls the sun and planets the *organs of time,* of which, independently of their stated revolutions, man could have formed no conception. The day is completed in twenty-four hours, during which space the earth moves round its axis, and express successively different parts of its surface to the sun. It goes at a rate of fifty-eight thousand miles an hour, and completes its orbit in the course of a year. (Haydock)

VERSE 16

Two great lights. God created on the first day *light,* which being moved from east to west, by its rising and setting made morning and evening. But on the fourth day he ordered and distributed this light, and made the sun, moon, and stars. The moon, though much less than the stars, is here called a *great light,* from its giving a far greater light to earth than any of them. (Challoner) --- *To rule* and adorn, for nothing appears so glorious as the sun and moon. (Menochius) --- Many have represented the stars, as well as the sun and moon, to be animated. Ecclesiastes xvi, speaking of the sun says, *the spirit goeth forward surveying all places:* and in Esdras ix. 6, the Levites address God, *Thou hast made heaven and all the host thereof; and thou givest life to all these things, and the host of heaven adoreth thee.* St. Augustine *Ench* and others, consider this question as not pertaining to faith. See Spencer in Origen, contra Cels. v. (Calmet) --- Whether the stars be the suns of other worlds, and whether the moon, &c. be inhabited, philosophers dispute, without being able to come to any certain conclusion: for *God has delivered the world to their consideration for dispute, so that man cannot find out the work which God hath made from the beginning to the end,* Ecclesiastes. iii. 11. If we must frequently confess our ignorance concerning the things which surround us, how shall we pretend to dive into the designs of God, or subject the mysteries of faith to our feeb... ...n! If we think the Scriptures really contradict the systems of philosophers, ought we to pay greater deference to the latter, than to the unerring word of God? But we must remember, that the sacred writings were given to instruct us in the way to heaven, and not to unfold to us the systems of natural history; and hence God generally addresses us in a manner best suited to our conceptions, and speaks of nature as it appears to the generality of mankind. At the same time, we may confidently asset, that the Scriptures never assert what is false. If we judge, with the vulgar, that the sun, moon, and stars are no larger than they appear to our naked eye, we shall still have sufficient reason to admire the works of God; but, if we are enabled to discover that the sun's diameter, for example, is 763 thousand miles, and its distance from our earth about 95 million miles, and the fixed stars (as they are called, though probably all in motion) much more remote, what astonishment must fill our breast! Our understanding is bewildered in the unfathomable abyss, in the unbounded expanse, even of the visible creation. --- Sirius, the nearest to us of all the fixed stars, is supposed to be 400,000 times the distance from the sun that our earth is, or 38 millions of millions of miles. Light, passing at the rate of twelve millions of miles every minute, would be nearly 3,000 years in coming to us from the remotest star in our stratum, beyond which are others immensely distant, which it would require about 40,000 years to reach, even with the same velocity. Who shall not then admire thy works and fear thee, O King of ages! (Walker.) --- Geog. justly remarks, "we are lost in wonder when we attempt to comprehend either the vastness or minuteness of creation. Philosophers think it possible for the universe to be reduced to the smallest size, to an atom, merely by filling up the pores;" and the reason they allege is, "because we know not the real structure of bodies." Shall any one then pretend to wisdom, and still call in question the mysteries of faith, transubstantiation, &c., when the most learned confess they cannot fully comprehend the nature even of a grain of sand? While on the one hand some assert, that all the world may be reduced to this compass; others say, a grain of sand may be divided *in infinitum!* (Haydock)

VERSE 20

Creeping: destitute of feet like fishes, which move on their bellies. (Menochius) --- *Fowl.* Some assert that birds were formed of the earth, but they seem to have the same origin as fishes, namely, water; and still they must not be eaten on days of abstinence, which some of the ancients thought lawful, Socrates v. 20. To conciliate the two opinions, perhaps we might say, that the birds were formed of mud, (Calmet) or that some of the nature of fish, like barnacles, might be made of water and others of earth, chap. 11, 19. --- *Under:* Hebrew: on the face of the firmament, or in the open air. (Haydock)

VERSE 22

Blessed them, or enabled them to produce others. --- *Multiply:* the immense numbers and variety of fishes and fowls is truly astonishing.

VERSE 26

Let us make man to our image. This *image* of God in man, is not in the body, but in the soul; which is a *spiritual* substance, endued with understanding and free-will. God speaketh here in the plural number, to insinuate the plurality of *persons* in the Deity. (Challoner) --- Some of the ancient Jews maintained that God here addressed his council, the Angels; but is it probable that he should communicate to them the title of Creator, and a perfect similitude with himself? (Calmet) --- Man is possessed of many prerogatives above all other creatures of this visible world: his soul gives him a sort of equality with the Angels; and though his body be taken from the earth, like the brutes, yet even here the beautiful construction, the head erect and looking towards heaven, &c. makes St. Augustine observe, an air of majesty in the human body, which raises man above all terrestrial animals, and brings him in some measure near to the Divinity. As Jesus assumed our human nature, we may assert, that we bear a resemblance to God both in soul and body. Tertullian (de Resur. 5) says, "Thus that slime, putting on already the image of Christ, who would come in the flesh, was not only the work of God, but also a pledge." (Haydock) See St. Bernard on Psalm xcix. (Worthington)

VERSE 27

Male and female. Eve was taken from Adam's side on this same day, though it be related in the following chapter. Adam was not an hermaphrodite as some have foolishly asserted. (Calmet) --- *Adam* means *the likeness,* or *red earth,* that in one word we may behold our nobility and meanness. (Haydock)

VERSE 28

Increase and multiply. This is not a precept, as some protestant controvertists would have it, but a blessing, rendering them fruitful: for God had said the same words to the *fishes and birds,* (ver. 22.) who were incapable of receiving a precept. (Challoner) --- *Blessed them,* not only with fecundity as he had done to other creatures, but also with dominion over them, and much more with innocence and abundance of both natural and supernatural gifts. ---

Increase. The Hebrews understand this literally as a precept binding every man at twenty years of age (Calmet); and some of the Reformers argued hence, that Priests, &c. were bound to marry: very prudently they have not determined how soon! But the Fathers in general agree that if this were a precept with respect to Adam, for the purpose of *filling the earth,* it is no longer so, that end being sufficiently accomplished. Does not St. Paul wish all men to be like himself, *unmarried?* (1 Corinthians vii. 1, 7, 8.) (Haydock)

VERSE 29

Every herb, &c. As God does not here express leave to eat flesh-meat, which he did after the deluge, it is supposed that the more religious part of mankind, at least, abstained from it, and from wine, till after that event, when they became more necessary to support decayed nature. (Haydock) (Menochius) --- In the golden age, spontaneous fruits were the food of happy mortals. (Calmet)

CHAPTER II

VERSE 1

Furniture, ornaments or militia, whether we understand the Angels, or the stars, which observe a regular order and obey God. (Menochius)

VERSE 2

He rested, &c. That is, he ceased to make any new kinds of things. Though, as our Lord tells us, John v. 17. *He still worketh,* viz. by conserving and governing all things, and creating souls. (Challoner) ---*Seventh day.* This day was commanded, Exodus xx. 8, to be kept holy by the Jews, as it had probably been from the beginning. Philo says, it is the festival of the universe, and Josephus asserts, there is no town which does not acknowledge the religion of the Sabbath. But this point is controverted, and whether the ancient patriarchs observed the seventh day, or some other, it is certain they would not fail, for any long time, to show their respect for God's worship, and would hardly suffer a whole week to elapse without meeting to sound forth his praise. The setting aside of stated days for this purpose, is agreeable to reason, and to the practice of all civilized nations. As the Hebrews kept Saturday holy, in honor of God's rest, so we keep the first day of the week, by apostolic tradition, to thank God for the creation of the world on that day, and much more for the blessings which we derive from the Resurrection of Jesus Christ and the sending down of the Holy Ghost, which have given it a title above all other days.

(Haydock) *On the seventh day,* at the beginning of this verse, must be taken exclusively, as God finished his work on the 6th, whence the same Septuagint and Syriac have here *on the 6th day.* (Haydock) --- But the Hebrew and all the other versions agree with the Vulgate. (Calmet) --- The similarity of ver. 6 and ver. 7 in Hebrew may have given rise to this variation. (Haydock)

VERSE 4

Day. Not that all things were made in one day: but God formed in succession; first, heaven and earth, then the ornaments of both. *Every plant,* &c. which on the first day did not spring up, (as *water* covered the *surface of the earth,*) on the 3rd, by the command of God, without having any man to plant, or rain to water them, pushed forth luxuriantly, and manifested the power of the Creator. (Haydock) --- Thus Christ founded his Church by his own power, and still gives her increase; but requires of his ministers to co-operate with him, as a gardener must now take care of the plants which originally grew without man's aid. (Du Hamel) --- By observing that all natural means were here wanting for the production of plants, God asserts his sole right to the work, and confounds the Egyptian system, which attributed plants, &c. to the general warmth of the earth alone. (Calmet)

VERSE 7

Breath of life or a soul, created out of nothing, and infused into the body to give it life. (Haydock)

VERSE 8

Of pleasure, Hebrew *Eden,* which may be either the name of a country, as chap. iv. 16 or it may signify pleasure, in which sense Symmachus and St. Jerome have taken it. --- *From the beginning,* or on the 3rd day, when all plants were created, Hebrew *mikedem,* may also mean *towards the east,* as the Septuagint have understood it, though the other ancient interpreters agree with St. Jerome. Paradise lay probably to the east of Palestine, or of that country where Moses wrote. The precise situation cannot be ascertained. Calmet places it in Armenia, others near Babylon, &c. Some assert that this beautiful garden is still in being, the residence of Henoch and Elias. But God will not permit the curiosity of man to be gratified by the discovery of it, chap. iii. 24. How great might be its extent we do not know. If the sources of the Ganges, Nile, Tigris, and Euphrates, be not now changed, and if these be the rivers which sprung from the fountains of Paradise, (both which are points undecided) the garden must have comprised a great part of the world, (Haydock), as the Ganges rises in Judea [India], and the Nile about the middle of Africa. (Tirinus)

VERSE 9

The tree of life. So called, because it had that quality that by eating of the fruit of it, man would have been preserved in a constant state of health, vigor, and strength, and would not have died at all. *The tree of knowledge.* To which the deceitful serpent falsely attributed the power of imparting a superior kind of knowledge beyond that which God was pleased to give. (Challoner) --- Of what species these two wonderful trees were, the learned are not agreed. The *tree of knowledge,* could not communicate any wisdom to man; but, by eating of its forbidden fruit, Adam dearly purchased the knowledge of evil, to which he was before a stranger. Some say it was the fig-tree, others an apple-tree, Canticle of Canticles viii. 5. But it probably agreed with no species of trees with which we are acquainted, nor was there perhaps any of the same kind in paradise. (Tirinus)

VERSE 10

A river, &c. Moses gives many characteristics of Paradise, inviting us, as it were, to search for it; and still we cannot certainly discover where it is, or whether it exist at all at present, in state of cultivation. We must therefore endeavor to find the mystic Paradise, Heaven and the true Church; the road to which, though more obvious, is too frequently mistaken.

VERSE 15

To dress it. Behold God would not endure idleness even in Paradise. (Haydock)

VERSE 17

The death of the soul, and become obnoxious to that of the body; thou shalt become a mortal and lose all the privileges of innocence. Though Adam lived 930 years after this, he was dying daily; he carried along with him the seeds of death, as we do, from our very conception. He had leave to eat of any fruit in this delicious garden, one only excepted, and this one prohibition makes him more eager to taste of that tree than of all the rest. So we struggle constantly to attain what is forbidden, and covet what is denied, *cupimusque negata.* God laid this easy command upon Adam, to give him an opportunity of showing his ready obedience, and to assert his own absolute dominion over him. Eve was already formed, and was apprised of this positive command, (chap. iii) and therefore, transgressing, is justly punished with her husband. True obedience does not inquire *why* a thing is commanded, but submits without demur. Would a parent be satisfied with his child, if he should refuse to obey, because he could not discern the propriety of the restraint? If he should forbid him to touch some delicious fruits which he had reserved for strangers, and the child were to eat them, excusing himself very impertinently and blasphemously, with those much abused words of our Savior, *It is not what enters into the mouth that defiles a man,* &c. would not even a Protestant parent be enraged and seize the rod, though he could not but see that he was thus condemning his own conduct, in disregarding, on the very same plea, the fasts and days of abstinence, prescribed by the Church and by God's authority? All meats are good, as that fruit most certainly was which Adam was forbidden to eat; though some have foolishly surmised that it was poisonous; but, the crime of disobedience draws on punishment. (Haydock) --- Even when the sin is remitted, as it was to Adam, the penalty is not of course released, as some have pretended. This also clearly appears in baptized infants, who suffer the penalties due to original sin, as much as those who have not been admitted to the laver of regeneration. (St. Augustine; Worthington; Tirinus, &c.) --- If on this occasion, Eve had alone transgressed, as she was not the head, her sin would have hurt only herself. But with Adam, the representative of all his posterity, God made a sort of compact, giving him to understand, that if he continued faithful, his children should be born in the state of innocence like himself, happy and immortal, to be translated in due time to a happier Paradise, &c. but if he should refuse to obey, his sin should be communicated to all his race, who should be, *by nature, children of wrath.* --- (St. Augustine, City of God xvi. 27; Ven. Bede in Luc. 11; &c.) --- (Haydock) (Calmet)

VERSE 20

Names, probably in the Hebrew language, in which the names of things, frequently designate their nature and quality.

VERSE 21

A deep sleep. Septuagint, "an ecstasy," or mysterious sleep, in which Adam was apprised of the meaning of what was done, and how the Church would be taken from the side of Christ, expiring on the cross. (Menochius)

VERSE 23

Of my flesh. God did not, therefore, take a rib without flesh, nor perhaps did he replace flesh without a rib in Adam's side, though St. Augustine thinks he did. These words of Adam are attributed to God, Matthew xix, because they were inspired by him. --- *Woman.* As this word is derived from man, so in Hebrew *Isha* (or *Asse*) comes from *Iish* or *Aiss*; Latin *vira* woman, and *virago* comes from *vir*. (Haydock) --- But we do not find this allusion so sensible in any of the Oriental languages, as in the Hebrew, whence another proof arises of this being the original language. (Calmet)

VERSE 24

One flesh, connected by the closest ties of union, producing children, the blood of both. St. Paul, Ephesians v. 23, discloses to us the mystery of Christ's union with his church for ever, prefigured by this indissoluble marriage of our first parents. (Calmet)

VERSE 25

Not ashamed, because they had not perverted the work of God. Inordinate concupiscence is the effect of sin. (Haydock)

CHAPTER III
VERSE 1

Why hath God? Hebrew, "Indeed hath God, &c." as if the serpent had overheard Eve arguing with herself, about God's prohibition, with a sort of displeasure and presumption. St. Augustine thinks, she had given some entrance to these passions, and the *love of her own power*, and hence gave credit to the words of the serpent, de Gen. ad lit. xi. 30. She might not know or reflect that the serpent could not reason thus, naturally; and she had as yet, no idea or dread of the devil. (Lombard, 2 Dist. 21.) This old serpent entered into the most subtle of creatures, and either by very expressive signs, or by the motion of the serpent's tongue, held this delusive dialogue with Eve. Moses relates what happened exteriorily; but from many expressions, and the curse, ver. 15, he sufficiently indicates, that an evil spirit was the latent actor. (Haydock) --- *Of every tree.* Satan perverts the word of God, giving it an ambiguous turn: in doing which, he has set heretics a pattern, which they follow. (Menochius)

VERSE 3

Not touch it. She exaggerates, through dislike of restraint, St. Ambrose. Or through reverence, she thought it unlawful to touch what she must not eat, *lest perhaps,* as if there could be any doubt. "God asserts, the woman doubts, Satan denies." (St. Bernard) Thus place, like Eve, between God and the devil, to whom shall we yield our assent? (Haydock) --- *Perhaps we die,* Hebrew, "lest ye die."

VERSE 5

God. The old serpent's aim is, to make us think God envies our happiness. (Haydock) --- Or he would have Eve to suppose, she had not rightly understood her maker, who would surely never deprive her of a fruit which would give her such an increase of knowledge, as to make her conclude she was before comparatively blind. (Menochius) --- *As gods,* Hebrew *Elohim,* which means also princes, angels, or judges. It appears, that our first parents had flattered themselves with the hopes of attaining a divine knowledge of all things. (Calmet)

VERSE 6

Woman saw, or gazed on with desire and fond dalliance. (Menochius) --- Consulting only her senses, which represented the fruit to her as very desirable, and caused her to give credit to the devil's insinuations, rather than to the express word of God. Do not unbelievers the like, when they refuse to admit the real presence and transubstantiation, thought they cannot be ignorant, that this way of proceeding always leads to ruin. --- *Her husband,* who, instead of reproving her for her rashness, *did eat,* through excessive fondness, not being able to plead ignorance, or that he was deceived. "Earth trembled from her entails, sky colored, and muttering thunder, some sad drops wept at completing the mortal sin." --- (Original, &c.; Paradise Lost, ix. 1000.) (Haydock) --- (Genesis ii. 14.) In what light so ever we consider the fault of this unhappy pair, it is truly enormous: the precept was so easy and just, the attempt to be like God in knowledge so extravagant, that nothing but pride could have suggested such woeful disobedience. *By the disobedience of one man many were made sinners,* Romans v. 19. This ruin of himself, and of all his posterity, Adam could not hide from his own eyes, chap. ii. 17. (Calmet)

VERSE 7

And the eyes, &c. Not that they were blind before, (for the *woman saw that the tree was fair to the eyes,* ver. 6.) nor yet that *their eyes were opened* to any more perfect knowledge of good; but only to the unhappy experience of having lost the *good* of original grace and innocence, and incurred the dreadful *evil* of sin. From whence followed a shame of their being naked; which they minded not before; because being now stripped of original grace, they quickly began to be subject to the shameful rebellions of the flesh. (Challoner) --- Behold the noble acquisition of experimental knowledge! This is supposed to have taken place about a week after they had enjoyed the sweets of innocence and of Paradise, that they might afterwards be moved to repentance, when they contrasted their subsequent misery with those few golden days. They saw that they had received a dreadful wound, even in their natural perfections, and that their soul was despoiled of grace, which, of themselves, they could never regain. O! what confusion must now have seized upon them! "Confounded long they say, as stricken mute." (Milton) --- (Haydock)

Aprons, or they interwove tender branches covered with leaves round their middle; a practice, which even the wild Indians and Americans observed, when they were discovered by Columbus. They will rise up in condemnation of those pretended civilized nations, who, like the Greeks, could wrestle or bathe quite naked, without any sense of shame. (Haydock) --- *Adam's fig-tree,* in Egypt, has leaves above a yard long, and two feet broad. (Calmet)

VERSE 8

Afternoon air. God's presence has often been indicated by an unusual wind. (3 Kings xix. 12; Act. ii. 2.) The sovereign judge will not suffer the day to pass over, without bringing our first parents to a sense of their fault. *They hid themselves,* loving *darkness* now, because *their works were evil.*

VERSE 9

Where. In what state have thy sins placed thee, that thou shouldst flee from thy God? (St. Ambrose, C. 14) Some think it was the Son of God who appeared on this occasion, St. Augustine; &c. or an Angel. (Calmet)

VERSE 10

Afraid. The just man is first to accuse himself: but Adam seeks for excuses in his sin: he throws the blame on his wife, and ultimately on God. (Menochius) --- *Thou gavest me.* Heretics have since treated the Sovereign Good with the like insolence; saying plainly, that God is the author of sin, and that the crime of Judas is no less his work than the conversion of St. Paul. See Calvin's works, and many of the first reformers, Luther, &c. cited.

VERSE 13

The serpent, which thou hast made so cunning, and placed with us, *deceived me.* God deigns not to answer their frivolous excuses. (Menochius)

VERSE 14

Cursed. This curse falls upon the natural serpent, as the instrument of the devil; who is also cursed at the same time by the Holy Ghost. What was natural to the serpent and to man in a state of innocence, (as to creep, &c. to submit to the dominion of the husband, &c.) becomes a punishment after the fall. (St. Chrysostom) --- There was no enmity, before, between man and any of God's creatures; nor were they noxious to him. (Tirinus) --- The devil seems now to crawl, because he no longer aspires after God and heavenly things, but aims at wickedness and mean deceit. (Menochius)

VERSE 15

She shall crush. Ipsa, the woman: so divers of the fathers read this place, conformably to the Latin: others read it *ipsum,* viz. the seed. The sense is the same: for it is by her seed, *Jesus Christ,* that the woman crushes the serpent's head. (Challoner) --- The Hebrew text, as Bellarmine observes, is ambiguous: He mentions one copy which had *ipsa* instead of *ipsum;* and so it is even printed in the Hebrew inter-lineary edition, 1572, by Plantin, under the inspection of Boderianus. Whether the Jewish editions ought to have more weight with Christians, or whether all the other manuscripts conspire against this reading, let others inquire. The fathers who have cited the old Italic version, taken from the Septuagint agree with the Vulgate, which is followed by almost all the Latins; and hence we may argue with probability, that the Septuagint and the Hebrew formerly acknowledged *ipsa,* which now moves the indignation of Protestants so much, as if we intended by it to give any divine honor to the blessed Virgin. We believe, however, with St. Epiphanius, that "it is no less criminal to vilify the holy Virgin, than to glorify her above measure." We know that all the power of the mother of God is derived from the merits of her Son. We are no otherwise concerned about the retaining of *ipsa,* she, in this place, that in as much as we have yet no certain reason to suspect its being genuine. As some words have been corrected in the Vulgate since the Council of Trent by Sixtus V and others, by Clement VIII so, if, upon stricter search, it be found that *it,* and not *she,* is the true reading, we shall not hesitate to admit the correction: but we must wait in the mean time respectfully, till our superiors determine. (Haydock) Kemnitzius certainly advanced a step too far, when he said that all the ancient fathers read *ipsum.* Victor, Avitus, St. Augustine, St. Gregory, &c mentioned in the Douay Bible, will convict him of falsehood. Christ crushed the serpent's head by his death, suffering himself to be wounded in the heel. His blessed mother crushed him likewise, by her cooperation in the mystery of the Incarnation; and by rejecting, with horror, the very first suggestions of the enemy, to commit even the smallest sin. (St. Bernard, ser. 2, on *Missus est.*) "We crush," says St. Gregory, Mor. 1. 38, "the serpent's head, when we extirpate from our heart the beginnings of temptation, and then he lays snares for our heel, because he opposes the end of a good action with greater craft and power." The serpent may hiss and threaten; he cannot hurt, if we resist him. (Haydock)

VERSE 16

And thy conceptions. Septuagint:"thy groaning." The multifarious sorrows of childbearing, must remind all mothers (the blessed Virgin alone excepted) of what they have incurred by original sin. If that had not taken place, they would have conceived without concupiscence, and brought forth without sorrow. (St. Augustine, City of God xiv. 26.)--- Conceptions are multiplied on account of the many *untimely* deaths, in our fallen state. *Power,* which will sometimes be exercised with rigor. (Haydock) --- Moses here shows the original and natural subjection of wives to their husbands, in opposition to the Egyptians, who, to honor Isis, gave women the superiority by the marriage contract. (Diodorus i. 2.) (Calmet)

VERSE 17

Thy work, sin; *thy perdition is from thyself:* this is all that man can challenge for his own. (Haydock)

VERSE 18

Thorns, &c. These were created at first, but they would have easily been kept under: now they grow with surprising luxuriance, and the necessaries of life can be procured only with much labor. All men here are commanded to work, each in his proper department. The Jews were careful to teach their children some trade or useful occupation. St. Paul made tents, and proclaims, *If any man will not work, neither let him eat,* 2 Thessalonians iii. 10. (Calmet)

VERSE 19

Dust, as to the visible part; and thy soul created out of nothing. This might serve to correct that pride, by which Adam had fallen; and the same humbling truths are repeated to us by the Church every Ash-Wednesday, to guard us against the same contagion, the worm of pride, to which we are all so liable. Thus Adam was again assured that he should die the death, with which God had threatened him, and which the devil had told Eve would not be inflicted, ver. 4. *God created man incorruptible, (inexterminabilem,* immortal). *But by the envy of the devil, death came into the world,* Wisdom ii. 23. (Haydock)

VERSE 20

The living. Hebrew *chai,* one who brings forth alive, (Symmachus) or one who imparts life, in which she was a figure of the blessed Virgin. (Calmet) --- Adam gives his wife this new name, in gratitude for not being cut off by death on the very day of his transgression, as he had every reason to expect and fear he would have been (Haydock) --- The printed Hebrew reads here, and in many other place, *Eva, he,* instead of *Eja, she;* thus, *He was the mother,* ver. 12, *he gave,* &c. an inaccuracy unknown to the Samaritan and the best manuscripts copies. (Kennicott)

VERSE 21

Of skins, which Adam took from the beasts which he offered in sacrifice to his merciful Judge, testifying thereby that he had forfeited his life, and uniting himself to that sacrifice of the woman's promised seed, by which alone he believed the sin of the world was to be expiated. (Haydock)

VERSE 22

Behold Adam, &c. This was spoken by way of reproaching him with his pride, in affecting a knowledge that might make him like to God. (Challoner) --- "These are the words of God, not insulting over man, but deterring others from an imitation of his pride." (St. Augustine, de Gen. xi. 39.) --- *For ever.* The sentence is left imperfect: (Calmet) but by driving man from Paradise, God sufficiently showed how he would prevent from eating of the tree of life, (Haydock) which Adam had not yet found. As he was now condemned to be miserable on earth, God, in mercy, prevented him from tasting of that fruit, which would have rendered his misery perpetual. (Menochius) --- He would suffer him to die, that, by death, he might come, after a life of 930 years, spent in sorrow and repentance, to the enjoyment of himself. (Haydock) ---*Lest perhaps.* God does not exercise his absolute power, or destroy free-will, but makes use of ordinary means and precautions, to effect his designs. (St. Augustine) (Worthington)

VERSE 24

Cherubims. Angels of the highest order, and of a very complex figure, unlike any one living creature. Theodoret supposes that God forced Adam to retire from that once charming abode, by the apparition of hideous specters. The devils were also hindered from coming hither, lest they should pluck the fruit of the tree of life, and by promising immortality, should attract men to their service. *The flaming sword* might be a fire rising out of the earth, of which Grotius thinks the pits, near Babylon, are still vestiges. These dreadful indications of the divine wrath would probably disappear, when Paradise had lost its superior beauty, and become confounded with the surrounding countries --- Thus we have seen how rapidly Moses describes the creation of all things, the fall of man, and the promised redemption. But in these few lines, we discover a solution of the many difficulties which have perplexed the learned, respecting these most important subjects. We know that the world is not the effect of chance, but created and governed by divine Providence. We are no longer at the loss to explain the surprising contrast of good and evil, observable in the same man. When we have attentively considered the Old Adam and the New, we find a clue to lead us through all the labyrinths of our Holy Religion. We could wish, perhaps, for a greater detail in Moses, but he left the rest to be supplied by tradition. He has thrown light enough upon the subjects, to guide the well-disposed, and has left sufficient darkness to humble and to confound the self-conceited and wicked, who loved darkness rather than the light. (Calmet) --- Concerning the transactions of these early times, parents would no doubt be careful to instruct their children, by word of mouth, before any of the Scriptures were written; and Moses might derive much information from the same source, as a very few persons formed the chain of tradition, when they lived so many hundred years. *Adam* would converse with *Mathusalem,* who knew *Sem,* as the latter lived in the days of *Abram. Isaac, Joseph,* and *Amram,* the father of *Moses,* were contemporaries: so that seven persons might keep up the memory of things which had happened 2500 years before. But to entitle these accounts to absolute authority, the inspiration of God intervenes; and thus we are convinced, that no word of sacred writers can be questioned. (Haydock)

CHAPTER IV
VERSE 1

Through God. Hebrew may signify also: "even God," as if she thought this was the promised seed, who, as Onkelos paraphrases it, would serve the Lord. (Calmet) --- So little could she foresee the future conduct of Cain, whose name may be derived either from *kone, possession* and *acquisition,* or from *kun, lamentation.* The latter interpretation would have been better verified by the event, and the name of Abel, *vanity,* or *sorrow,* for which his parents allege no reason, might also have been reversed, on account of his justice, for which he is canonized by Christ himself, and declared *the Just.* Pious and significant names were imposed by either parent. Cain was the second man. He was not conceived till after the fall, and was therefore the first born in original sin. (Haydock)

VERSE 4

Had respect. That is, showed his acceptance of his sacrifice (as coming from a heart full of devotion) and that we may suppose, by some visible token, such as sending fire from heaven upon his offerings. (Challoner) --- The offerings of Cain are mentioned without any approbation: those of Abel are the *firstlings* and *fat,* or the very best; by which he testified, that he acknowledged God for his first beginning. Sacrifice is due to God alone, and to Him it has always been offered in the Church. We have the happiness to offer that truly Eucharistic sacrifice to God, of which those of ancient times were only figures. What sacrifice can our erring brethren show? (Worthington; Calmet)

VERSE 7

Over it. This is a clear proof of free-will. To destroy its force, Protestants translate *over him,* as if Cain should still retain his privilege of the first-born, notwithstanding all his wickedness, and should rule over Abel, who would willingly submit, "unto thee his desire," &c. But God had made no mention of Abel. The whole discourse is about doing well or ill; and Cain is encouraged to avoid the stings of conscience, by altering his conduct, as it was in his power, how strongly so ever his passions might solicit him to evil. (Haydock) --- The Hebrew is understood by Onkelos, and the Targum of Jerusalem, in the sense of the Vulgate. The latter reads, "If thou correct thy proceedings in this life, thou wilt receive pardon in the next world. But if thou do not penance for thy sin, it shall remain till the day of the great judgment, and it shall stay, lying at the door of thy heart. But I have given thee power to govern thy concupiscence: thou shalt sway it, either to embrace good or evil." Calmet shows that the Hebrew perfectly admits of this sense. St. Augustine will not allow of the turn which the Manichees gave it. "Thou shalt have dominion over (*illius.*) What? thy brother! (*absit*) by no means: over what then, but sin? (City of God xv. 7.) Protestants formerly abandoned the translation of 1579, (which they have again resumed) and translated better, "unto thee shall be the desire thereof, and thou shalt rule over it," which R. Abenezra explains also of sin. To which of these editions, all given by royal authority, will Protestants adhere? Luther wrote a book against free-will, and Calvin would not admit the very name. But we, with all antiquity, must cry out with St. Jerome, contra Jov. 2: "God made us with free-will, neither are we drawn by necessity to virtue or vice; else where there is necessity, there is neither damnation nor reward." (Worthington; Haydock)

VERSE 8

Let us go forth abroad. These words are now wanting in the Hebrew; being omitted, according to Kennicott, since the days of Aquila 130; they are found in the Samaritan copy and version, in the Septuagint, &c. (Haydock) --- The Masorets place a mark, as if something were defective here, and in 27 other verses, or in 25 at least. (Haydock) --- Abel's violent death was a figure of that of Jesus Christ, inflicted for the like cause. See Hebrews xii. 2. (Calmet) --- In consequence of these crimes, Cain separated from the Church, and the Jews became no longer God's people: both Cain and the Jews became vagabonds. (Haydock) --- The Targum of Jerusalem observes, that Cain talked against God's providence and the future world, which Abel hearing with marked indignation, Cain took occasion to kill him. (Worthington)

VERSE 13

My iniquity, &c. Like Judas, Cain despairs. The Rabbins make him complain of the rigor of God's judgment, "My sin (or punishment) is too great to be borne." I must then be driven from the land of my nativity, from the society of my brethren and parents, from thy presence, forever. Why do I then live? Let the first man I meet, kill me. (Liranus)

VERSE 14

Every one that findeth me, shall kill me. His guilty conscience made him fear his own brothers, and nephews; of whom, by this time, there might be a good number upon the earth: which had now endured near 130 years; as may be gathered from Genesis v. 3, compared with chap. iv. 25, though in the compendious account given in the Scripture, only Cain and Abel are mentioned. (Challoner) --- Cain is little concerned about anything but the loss of life. (Menochius)

VERSE 15

Set a mark, &c. The more common opinion of the interpreters of holy writ, supposes this mark to have been a trembling of the body; or a horror and consternation in his countenance. (Challoner) --- God gave this first murderer a reprieve, allowing him time for repentance; but he neglected it, and died a reprobate; having been, during life, the head of an apostate church, and of the city of the devil, which has ever since opposed the city of God, and the society of the faithful. Though all his posterity were drowned in the deluge, some were soon found, even in the family of Noe, who stood up for the wretched pre-eminence in wickedness and rebellion, against the truth. See St. Augustine; Worthington; &c. (Haydock)

VERSE 16

A fugitive, according to his sentence. Hebrew *nod,* which the Septuagint have taken for a proper name. "In the land of Naid, over against Eden," (Haydock) or in the fields of *Nyse,* in Hyrcania, to the east of Eden and Armenia. (Calmet)

VERSE 17

His wife. She was a daughter of Adam, and Cain's own sister; God dispensing with such marriages in the beginning of the world, as mankind could not otherwise be propagated. --- *He built a city,* viz. In process of time, when his race was multiplied, so as to be numerous enough to people it. For in the many hundred years he lived, his race might be multiplied even to millions. (Challoner) --- The Hanuchta, which Ptolemy places in Susiana, (Calmet) may perhaps have been built after the flood, in the same place. Josephus says, Cain was the first who fortified a city; designing it for a retreat, where he might keep the fruits of his robberies, Antiquities 1. 3. Peirere founds his ill-concerted system of *Preadamites,* or of men existing before Adam, on the history of Cain exercising husbandry, building a city, &c.; as if there were any difficulty in supposing, that the arts would have made some progress in the lapse of above a century. (Haydock)

VERSE 19

Two wives. Lamech first transgressed the law of having only one wife at a time. (chap. ii. 24.) None before the deluge is mentioned as having followed his example, even among the abandoned sons of men. Abraham, the father of the faithful, and some others, after that event, when the age of man was shortened, and the number of the true servants of God very small, were dispensed with by God, who tolerated the custom of having many wives at the same time among the Jews, till our Savior brought things back to the ancient standard. (Matthew xix. 4.) And why do we excuse the patriarchs, while we condemn Lamech? Because the one being associated with the wicked, gives us reason to judge unfavorably of him, while Abraham is constantly mentioned in Scripture with terms of approbation and praise, and therefore we have no right to pass sentence of condemnation upon him, as some Protestants have done, after the Manichees. Hence the fathers defend the one, and reject the other with abhorrence. (Haydock) --- Tertullian (Monog. c. 5.) and St. Jerome, contra Jovin. 1, says, "Lamech, first of all, a bloody murderer, divided one flesh between two wives." It was never lawful, says Pope Innocent III contra *Gaudemus,* for anyone to have many wives at once, unless leave was given by divine revelation;" and St. Augustine joins with him in defending the patriarchs, by this reason, "When it was the custom, it was not a sin."

VERSE 22

Noema, who is supposed to have invented the art of spinning. (Calmet) --- All these worthy people were distinguished for their proficiency in the arts, while they neglected the study of religion and virtue. (Haydock) --- The inventors of arts among the Greeks lived mostly after the siege of Troy. (Calmet)

VERSE 23

Said. This is the most ancient piece of poetry with which we are acquainted. (Fleury.) --- Lamech may be considered as the father of poets. (Haydock) --- *I have slain a man,* &c. It is the tradition of the Hebrews, that Lamech in hunting slew Cain, mistaking him for a wild beast: and that having discovered what he had done, he beat so unmercifully the youth, by whom he was led into that mistake, that he died of the blows. (Challoner) --- St. Jerome, 9. 1. ad Dam. acknowledges the difficulty of this passage, on which Origen wrote two whole books. (Worthington)

VERSE 24

Seventy times. A similar expression occurs, Matthew xviii. 22 to denote a great but indefinite number. God had promised to revenge the murder of Cain seven fold, though he had sinned voluntarily; so Lamech hopes that, as he had acted by mistake, and blinded by passion, in striking the stripling, the son of Tubalcain, he would deserve to be protected still more from falling a prey to the fury of any other. But many reject this tradition as fabulous, unknown to Philo, Josephus, &c. Moses nowhere mentions the death of Cain. Some, therefore, understand this passage with an interrogation; as if, to convince his wives that his sin was not so enormous as was supposed, he should say, Do not think of leaving me. What! have I killed a young man, as Cain did Abel, and still he is suffered to live unmolested; or have I beaten any one so that I should be punished? Onkelos, in effect, puts a negation to the same purport, "I have not killed, &c.:" (Calmet) others understand this passage, as if Lamech considered his crimes as much more grievous than even those of Cain. (Tirinus)

VERSE 26

Began to call upon, &c. Not that Adam and Seth had not called upon God before the birth of Enos, but that Enos used more solemnity in the worship and invocation of God. (Challoner) --- He directed all his thoughts towards heaven, being reminded by his own name, which signifies one afflicted, that he could look for no solid happiness on earth. Seth had brought him up, from his infancy, in these pious sentiments, and his children were so docile to his instructions, that they began to be known in the world for their extraordinary piety, and were even styled the *Sons of God,* chap. vi. 2. (Haydock) --- Religion was not a human invention, but many ceremonies have been adopted, at different times, to make an impression on the minds of the people. Before Enos, the heads of families had officiated in their own houses; now, perhaps, they met together in places consecrated to the divine service, and sounded forth the praises of the Most High. Enos was probably most conspicuous for his zeal on these occasions: at least, a new degree of fervor manifested itself in his days. On the other hand, "the name of the Lord began to be profaned" about this time, as the Rabbin understand this passage, by the introduction of idolatry; which is a common effect of a dissolute life, which many began now to lead, Wisdom xiv. 12. (Calmet) --- *The beginning of fornication is the devising of idols.* We have, nevertheless, no certain proof of idols being introduced till many years after the deluge. (Haydock)

CHAPTER V

VERSE 2

Adam: the common name of mankind, made to *the likeness of God.* (Haydock)

VERSE 5

He died. Ecclesiasticus XIV 12, says very justly, *the covenant of this world* is, he *shall surely die.* God prolonged the lives of the patriarchs to a more advanced age, that the world might be sooner filled. Their constitution was then more excellent, the fruits of the earth more nourishing, &c. But the sole satisfactory reason for their living almost a thousand years, while we can hardly arrive at 70, is, because so it pleased God, in whose hands are all our lots. There is a great difference in the number of years assigned by the Hebrew and Vulgate, from that which the Samaritan copy mentions; and the Septuagint differs from both. Whether the difference be real, or only apparent, we shall not pretend to determine. The Church has not decided which system of chronology is the most accurate. In the Martyrology, she adopts that of the Septuagint and placed the birth of Christ in 5199, after Eusebius and Ven. Bede, though Riccioli calculates the Septuagint at 5634 years. (Haydock) --- Adam died penitent, as we are assured by the Holy Ghost, Wisdom X 2; and tradition affirms the same of Eve, insomuch that the heresy of the Encratites, who condemned our first parents to hell, was exploded with horror. (St. Epiphanius; St. Augustine, in hæres; Tirinus)

VERSE 24

Walked with God. Septuagint, "was pleasing to God," by continual recollection and watchfulness over himself. Thus he became perfect. ---*Was seen no more;* or, as St. Paul reads, after the Septuagint, *he was not found.* (Hebrews xi. 5.) --- *God took him* alive to some place unknown, which is commonly supposed to be Paradise, conformably to Ecclesiasticus xliv. 16, though in Greek we do not read Paradise. *Henoch pleased God, and was translated [into Paradise], that he may give repentance to the nations.* To him, that of Wisdom iv. 10 may be applied: *He was beloved, and living among sinners, he was translated.* He will come again, when the charity of many of his children, (for we all spring from him) shall have grown cold; and shall at last suffer death for opposing Antichrist. (Apocalypse xi.) (Haydock) --- "Though it be not an article of faith, whether Henoch be now in that Paradise, from which Adam and Eve were driven, or in some other delightful place; yet the holy Scriptures affirm, that God translated him alive, that he might not experience death," St. Chrysostom, hom. 21, with whom the other fathers agree, cited in the Douay Bible; so that it is a matter of surprise, how any Protestant can call it in question. He is the other witness, who will come with Elias, before the great day of the Lord, to perform the same office to the nations, as the latter will to the Jews. (Malachias iv) God preserves these two alive, perhaps to give us a striking proof how he could have treated Adam and his posterity, if they had not sinned; and also to confirm our hopes of immortality, when we shall have paid the debt of nature. (Worthington)

VERSE 29

Noe means *consolation,* or *repose.* After he had beheld the most dreadful catastrophe or disturbance that ever happened in the world, he settled mankind once more in the friendship of God, and merited a blessing both for himself and for the whole earth. He gave, likewise, comfort to all, by useful inventions in agriculture, and in the art of making wine. He saw an end of the distractions caused by the wicked sons of Cain, and became the restorer of a new world: in a word, he was the progenitor of the Messias, who is the King of Peace, and our only solid comfort. (Menochius) (Haydock)

VERSE 31

Old. It is wonderful if Noe had no children before this time; but he might have had many, whom the Scripture does not mention, either because they were dead before the deluge, or taking evil courses with the daughters of men, deserved to perish with them. Noe kept the three, who were born after God had foretold the deluge, with the greatest care, under his own eyes. St. Augustine (City of God xv. 20.) thinks, however, that many of the Patriarchs had no children till they were pretty far advanced in years. As Sem was born when Noe was 502, and Cham was the youngest, Japheth must have been the first-born. Compare Chap. x. 21, with Chap. ix. 24. There is no reason to suppose they were all born the same year. (Calmet)

CHAPTER VI

VERSE 1

Daughters. These had borne equal proportion with the males from the beginning; but here they are particularized, because they were the chief instruments in corrupting the descendants of Seth. (Haydock) --- Even the sons of these libidinous people were so effeminate, as to deserve to be called women. (Menochius)

VERSE 2

The sons of God. The descendants of Seth and Enos are here called *Sons of God,* from their religion and piety: whereas the ungodly race of Cain, who by their carnal affections lay groveling upon the earth, are called the children of men. The unhappy consequence of the former marrying with the latter, ought to be a warning to Christians to be very circumspect in their marriages; and not to suffer themselves to be determined in choice by their carnal passion, to the prejudice of virtue or religion. (Challoner) --- See St. Chrysostom, hom. 22, &c. Some copies of the Septuagint having *the angels of God,* induced some of the ancients to suppose, that these spiritual beings (to whom, by another mistake, they attributed a sort of aerial bodies) had commerce with women, as the pagans derived their heroes from a mortal and a god. But this notion, which is borrowed from the book of Henoch, is quite exploded. (Calmet) --- The distinction of the true Church from the synagogue of Satan, here established, has been ever since retained, as heretics are still distinguished from Catholics. (Worthington) (St. Augustine)

VERSE 3

His days shall be, &c. The meaning is, that man's days, which before the flood were usually 900 years, should now be reduced to 120 years. Or rather, that God would allow men this term of 120 years, for their repentance and conversion, before he would send the deluge. (Challoner) --- He spoke therefore to Noe in his 480th year. (St. Augustine) --- Those who suppose, that he foretold this event 20 years later, think with St. Jerome, that God retrenched 20 years from the time first assigned for penance. The *Spirit* of the sovereign Judge was fired with *contending;* or, as others translate it, with remaining quiet as in a *scabbard,* and bearing with the repeated crimes of men. He resolved to punish them severely in this world, that he might show mercy to some of them hereafter. (St. Jerome, 9. Heb.) (Calmet) --- If we suppose, that God here threatens to reduce the space of man's life to 120 years, we must say, at least, that he did it by degrees; for many lived several hundred years, even after the deluge. In the days of Moses, indeed, few exceeded that term. But we think the other interpretation is more literal, and that God bore with mankind the full time which he promised. (Worthington)

VERSE 4

Giants. It is likely the generality of men before the flood were of a gigantic stature, in comparison with what men now are. But these here spoken of, are called *giants,* as being not only tall in stature, but violent and savage in their dispositions, and mere monsters of cruelty and lust. (Challoner) --- Yet we need not imagine, that they were such as the poets describe, tearing up mountains, and hurling them against heaven. Being offspring of men, who had lived hitherto with great temperance, but now gave full scope to their passions, and the love of the fair daughters whom *they chose,* we need not wonder that they should be amazingly strong and violent. *Nephilim, rushing on,* as Ag. translates. That there have been giants of an unusual size, all historians testify. Og, Goliah [Goliath], &c. are mentioned in Scripture, and the sons of Enac are represented as much above the common size, as the Hebrews were greater than grasshoppers, Numbers xiii. 34. If we should suppose they were four or five times our size, would that be more wonderful that they should live nine or ten times as long as we do? See St. Augustine, City of God xv. 9, 23; Calmet's Dissert. &c. Delrio affirms, that in 1572 he saw at Rouen, a native of Piedmont, above nine feet high. (Haydock) --- *Of old.* The corruption of morals had commenced many ages ago, and some of the sons of Seth had given way to their lusts; so that we are not to suppose, that these giants were all born within a hundred years of the flood, as some might suppose from their being mentioned here, after specifying the age of Noe, chap. v. 31. (Haydock)

VERSE 5

At all times. Hebrew only evil continually. They had no relish for anything else as we may say of a glutton, he thinks of nothing but his belly. Yet some good thoughts would occur occasionally, and we may grant that they did some things which were not sinful. (Menochius) --- If we follow corrupt nature, and live among sinners, we find a law within us warring against the spirit; and a very powerful grace is necessary to rescue us from such a dangerous situation. (Calmet) --- Though the expressions in this place seem general, they must be understood with some limitations. (Worthington)

VERSE 6

It repented him, &c. God, who is unchangeable, is not capable of repentance, grief, or any other passion. But these expressions are used to declare the enormity of the sins of men, which was so provoking as to determine their Creator to destroy these his creatures, whom before he had so much favored. (Challoner) --- God acted outwardly as a man would do who repented. (Haydock)

VERSE 8

Grace. Notwithstanding the general denunciation against all flesh, we see here that God will not confound the just with the guilty, in the same punishment. Noe pleased God, by observing the most perfect justice, in the midst of a corrupt generation. (St. Chrysostom; &c.) (Worthington)

VERSE 12

Its way, being abandoned to the most shameful and unnatural sins. (Liranus)

VERSE 13

All flesh. I will destroy all these carnal and wicked people, and, because all other creatures were made only for man's use, and will be useless, I will involve them in the common ruin, reserving only what will be necessary for the support of the few who shall be preserved, and for the re-peopling of the earth. (Haydock)

VERSE 14

Timber planks. Hebrew, "gopher wood," which is nowhere else mentioned in Scripture. It was probably a sort of wood full of rosin, and being besmeared with something like our pitch, was capable of resisting the fury of the ensuing tremendous storm, for a length of time. (Calmet; Haydock) --- *Rooms* to separate the birds, various animals, provisions, &c. --- *Pitch,* literally: "besmear it with bitumen," which has a very strong smell, able to counteract the disagreeable odors arising from beasts confined. (Menochius) --- It might be mixed with some other ingredients, naphtha, pitch, &c. (Calmet)

VERSE 15

Three hundred cubits, &c. The ark, according to the dimensions here set down, contained four hundred and fifty thousand square cubits; which were more than enough to contain all the kinds of living creatures, with all necessary provisions: even supposing the cubits here spoken of to have been only a foot and a half each, which was the least kind of cubits. (Challoner) --- It is therefore unnecessary for us to have recourse, with Cappel, to the sacred cubit, which was twice as large as the common one, but which seems not to have been in use among the Jews before the Babylonian captivity. Still less need we adopt the geometrical cubit, which contains six ordinary ones, as we might be authorized to do by the great names of Origen and St. Augustine, City of God xv. 27. q. in Gen. i. 4. These dimensions would make the ark as large as a city. Moses always speaks of the same sort of cubit, used probably in Egypt. Apelles and other heretics, with some modern infidels, have attempted to show, that this account of Moses is fabulous. But they have been amply refuted by able calculators, John Buteo, Pelletier, &c. This amazing structure, for which God himself gave the plan, was divided with three stories, besides the lower part of the vessel, which might serve to keep fresh water. The different species of animals are not so numerous, as some imagine. Fishes, and such creatures as can live in water, would not need to come into the ark. Animals deprived of exercise, and allowed barely what may support nature, will live upon a very little. Even an ox, according to Columella, will live on 30 pounds of hay, or on a cubic foot, a whole day, so that 400 of these large creatures might be supported on 146,000 cubic feet. The middle story, for provisions, would alone contain 150,000 cubits. Noe's family, and the birds, would probably occupy the room above, in which was a window all around, of the height of a *cubit,* without glass or crystal, which were not yet invented, but defended with lattice work of wood, like our dairy rooms. (Haydock)

VERSE 16

In a cubit. This is understood by some, of the height of the window; by others, of the roof, which would be almost flat, like the top of a coach. Menoch supposes, that the whole ark was to be measured with the cubit in every part, from the bottom *to the top;* and the words *of it,* properly refer to the ark. --- *Side,* or at the end, about the middle way, that the animals might be conveyed easily to their stalls. The door would open into the story allotted to the beasts, and all things might enter it by a sort of bridge, or by sloping planks. (Calmet) --- Ordure might be thrown down into the lowest part of the ark, separated from the reservoir of fresh water, or might be brought up with ropes and buckets to the window at the top, which would easily open. (Tirinus)

VERSE 18

My covenant, that thou shalt be saved, amid the general ruin. This is the second covenant of God with men: the first was with Adam, the third with Abraham, when circumcision was instituted, and the last with Moses, Exodus xix. All others were only ratifications of these; and even these were only figures of that which our Savior entered into with men, when he undertook to make satisfaction for them to his Father. (Calmet)

Two, intended for the propagation of their kind. God afterwards specifies what more Noe should preserve for food, chap. vii. 2. (Calmet). --- Wild beasts forgot their savage nature, and became subject to the just Noe; and all came readily at his beck, in the same manner as domestic animals come when we offer them food. Yet, in all this we must acknowledge the work of God, and a sort of miracle. (Haydock)

CHAPTER VII
VERSE 2

Of all clean. The distinction of clean and unclean beasts, appears to have been made before the law of Moses, which was not promulgated till the year of the world 2514. (Challoner). --- *Clean:* not according to the law of Moses, which was not yet given, but such as tradition had described --- fit for sacrifice; (Menochius) though they might be of the same species as were deemed clean in the law, which ratified the ancient institution. --- *And seven:* (Hebrew) simply *seven,* three couple and an odd female, for sacrifice after the deluge: one couple was to breed, the other two perhaps for food. (Haydock) --- Some imagine that there were fourteen unclean and four clean animals, of every species, in the ark, because the Samaritan, Septuagint, and Vulgate read, "seven and seven." (Origen, &c.) --- But our Savior, sending the Disciples to preach *two and two,* did not appoint a company of four to go together, but only of two, as is generally allowed, Mark vi. 7. (Calmet)

VERSE 11

Seventeenth day. On the tenth, God had given the last warning to the wretched and obstinate sinners, to whom Noe had been preaching, both by word and by building the ark, for 120 years; all in vain. This *second month* is, by some, supposed to be the month of May; by others, that of November. Usher makes Noe enter the ark on the 18th December 1656. The waters decreased May 17, mountains appear July 31, he sends out the raven September 8, and leaves the ark December 29, after having remained in it a year and ten days, according to the antediluvian computation, or a full year of 365 days. The systems of those pretended philosophers, who would represent this flood as only partial, affecting the countries which were then inhabited, are all refuted by the plain narration of Moses. What part of the world could have been secure, when the waters prevailed fifteen cubits above the highest mountains? To give a natural cause only for this miraculous effect would be nugatory: but as waters covered the earth at first, so they surely might again, by the power of God. (Haydock) ---*Fountains and flood-gates*. These are the two natural causes which Moses assigns for the deluge, the waters below, and those above in the sky or firmament. Heaven is said to be shut when it does not rain, (Luke iv. 25.) so it is here *opened*, and flood-gates, or torrents of rain, pour down incessantly. But God attributes not the deluge to these causes alone; he sufficiently intimates that it would be miraculous, (ver. 4, *I will rain,*) and still more emphatically, chap. vi. 17, *Behold I*. Hebrew, "I, even I myself, do bring on a flood of waters." The idea which Moses give of the flood, corresponds with that which he before gave of chaos, when earth and water were undistinguished in one confusing mass, chap. i. 6. The Hebrews look upon it as a continual miracle, that the earth is not always deluged, being founded, as they represent it, on the waters, Jeremias v. 22. Calmet and others have proved, both from Scripture and from philosophical arguments, the universality of the deluge, against Isaac Vossius, &c. (Haydock)

VERSE 16

The Lord shut him in, by an angel besmearing the door with pitch, to prevent the waters from penetrating, while Noe did the like in the inside. (Calmet) --- Thus God supplies our wants when we are not able to provide for ourselves, and though he could do all by himself, yet he requires us to cooperate with him, and often makes use of secondary causes. (Worthington)

VERSE 24

Days: counting from the end of the forty days, when the deluge was at its height. (Calmet) --- In all the histories of past ages, there is nothing so terrible as this event. What became of all those myriads of human beings who perished on this occasion? We know not. Some have charitably supposed, that, although the far greater part perished everlastingly, a few *who had been incredulous* while Noe preached, opened their eyes at last, when it was too late to save their bodies, and by sincere repentance rescued their souls from the flames, and were consigned to do penance, for a time, in the other world. These heard the preaching of Jesus Christ, or believed in his redemption, while they were yet living, and so deserved to partake of his mercies, and joyfully beheld his sacred person when he came to visit them in their *prison* of purgatory. 1 Peter iii. 19, *He came and preached to those spirits that were in prison which had been sometime incredulous, when they waited for the patience of God in the days of Noe, when the ark was a building: wherein a few, that is eight souls, were saved* from drowning *by water. Whereunto baptism, being of the like form, now saves you also,* &c. See F. S. Bellarmine, &c. In these last words of St. Peter, we may also notice, that the ark was a figure of baptism, which is so necessary, that without its reception, or desire of it at least, no man can be saved. It is also a figure of the cross, and of the one true Church, as the Fathers remark, with St. Augustine, City of God xv. i; Menochius &c.; St. Gregory, hom. 12 in Ezech. &c. --- This is so striking that it deserves to be seriously considered. It was only *one,* though God could have ordered many smaller vessels to be made ready, perhaps with less inconvenience to Noe, that we might reflect, out of the Church the obstinate will surely perish. St. Jerome, ep. ad Dam.: In this ark *all* that were truly *holy,* and some imperfect, like Cham, were contained, clean beasts and unclean dwelt together, that we need not wonder if some Catholics be a disgrace to their name. The ark had different partitions, to remind us of the various *orders* of Clergy and Laity in the Church, with one chief governor, the Pope, like Noe in the ark. It was strong, visible, &c., and pitched all over with the durable cement, *bitumen,* and riding triumphant amid the storms, the envy of all who were out of it, till at last it settled upon a *rock.* So the Church is built on a rock, against which the gates of hell shall not prevail: she is not less obvious to the sincere seeker, than a city built on the top of the highest mountain, &c. We might here take a retrospective view of the chief occurrences and personages of the former world; we should observe the same order of the things from the beginning, --- the conflict of virtue and vice, the preservation of the true faith and worship of God among a few chosen souls, who preferred to be persecuted by worldlings, rather than to offend God. *They contended earnestly for the faith once delivered to the Saints,* to Adam and Eve, once innocent, and afterwards penitent. We behold original sin and the promised remedy for mankind; while the rebel angels are abandoned, without redress. There was kept up a communion of saints: sacrifice to the one God was performed generally by the heads of families, who were priests in the law of nature. Even Cain, though a bad man, through hypocrisy, chose to offer sacrifice before he had quite broken off from the society of the faithful, and resolved to become the father of all excommunicated persons, and of all secedes. (chap. iv. 16.) He was admonished by God that he had free will, and might merit a reward by a different conduct. His sentence, as well as that pronounced upon Adam, and upon all mankind, before the flood, reminds us of the particular and general judgment; as the translation of Henoch sets before us the happy state of the blessed, and the immortality, of which it was an earnest. See Douay Bible, where the chief mysteries of faith are pointed out as the creed of the Antediluvians. Even the Blessed Trinity was insinuated, or shown to them, at a distance, in various texts: the unity and indissolubility of marriage were clearly expressed; the true Church continued in Noe, while the chain of schematics and heretics was broken, and Cain's progeny destroyed. In this period of time, we may discover what the ancients so often describe respecting the four ages: --- the *golden* age is most perfectly found in Paradise; but only for a few days, or perhaps only a few hours, during which our first parents preserved their innocence. The *silver* age may have lasted rather longer, till the murder of Abel, or 128 years, when Cain began to disturb the peace of the world. From that time, till the giants make their appearance, we may reckon the age of *brass.* But that of *iron* had continued for many years before the flood. The like deterioration of morals we may discover after the deluge, and again after the renovation of the world, by the preaching of the gospel. For some time after these two great events, things bore a pleasing aspect; Noe was busy in offering sacrifice to God, Christians wee all one heart and one soul, enjoying all things in common, and God gave a blessing to the earth, and confirmed his covenant with men. Then Cham, Nemrod, and Babel appear, heresies in the new law break forth, and disturb the lovely harmony of mankind: but still a sufficient number preserve their integrity, till about the days of Abraham and Arius, in their respective periods, and may be said to have lived in the *silver* age, when compared with the *brazen* insolence of the great majority of those who came after. The *iron* age of these two periods, may be dated from the persecution of Epiphanes against the Jews, when so may apostatized from the faith, and from that much more terrible persecution which will be raised against Christians by Antichrist, the man of sin, (of which the former was a type) when the charity of many shall grow cold, and Christ will hardly find faith upon the earth. To that age may just be applied, those strong expressions of disapprobation which God made use of before the flood, chap. vi. 3, 6, 12. He will punish the crimes of that age with a deluge of *fire,* and say, *The end of all flesh is come before me,* &c., ver. 13. *Time shall be no longer,* Apocalypse x. 6. (Haydock)

CHAPTER VIII
VERSE 1

Remembered; not as if God had ever forgotten Noe, but he now shows his remembrance of him by the effects. (Menochius) --- *A wind,* literally *a spirit,* which St. Ambrose and Theodoret understood of the Holy Ghost, that, as he moved over the waters at first, (chap. i. 2.) to give them fecundity, and to exercise his power in establishing order, so he may show the same care and providence for this new world, emerging, like the former, from the waters. (Haydock) --- Most interpreters, however, understand this of a violent wind, (Proverbs xxv. 23; Exodus xiv. 21) a strong blast, such as was sent to divide the Red sea. (Menochius)

VERSE 3

And the waters returned, &c. St. Jerome on this passage remarks, "that all waters and torrents repair to the womb of the abyss, through the hidden veins of the earth," and by the abyss understands the sea: according to that of Ecclesiastes i. 7, *all the rivers run into the sea.* But as the sea itself, on this occasion, exceeded its limits, (otherwise its waters would not have been higher than the land) the sense perhaps confined to this, that the waters by degrees were diminished; as we may say of the inundations of land, that the waters are gone off, not by the regular course of ditches, but from the effects of the sun and winds which dry them up. (Estius)

VERSE 4

And the ark rested on the mountains of Armenia. The Hebrew word is *Ararat,* which also occurs in the 37th chap. of Isaias, and the 51st of Jeremias; for in these places our interpreter retained the Hebrew word, but in the 4th book of Kings, xix. 37, where the same history is related, it is translated *by the land of the Armenians.* (Estius) --- *Seventh month,* of the year, not of the deluge, as appears from ver. 13, &c. (Menochius). --- *Seven and twentieth.* So also the Septuagint, but the Hebrew, &c. have the 17th. It is not easy to decide which is right. On the seventeenth the waters only began to decrease, and some hence argue for the Vulgate, as they say it is not probable the ark would stop that very day. (Calmet) --- This, however, might be the only mean by which Noe could discern that the waters were abating. (Haydock) --- The ark being about fourteen cubits sunk in the water, might soon touch the summit of the highest mountains, such as Mt. Taurus, of which the *Ararat,* here mentioned in the Hebrew, a mountain of *Armenia,* forms a part, according to St. Jerome. The Armenians still boast that they have the remains of the ark. Berosus, the Pagan historian, says bitumen was taken from it as a preservative. (Josephus, Antiquities i. 3; Eusebius, præp. ix. 4.) The Chaldee has Cordu for Ararat, whence some have supposed, that the ark rested on the Cordyean or Gordiean mountains. The Armenians call the mountain near Erivan, *Mesesonsar,* or the mountain of the ark. (Calmet)

VERSE 7

Did not return. The negotiation *Not,* is not to be found in any Hebrew copy now extant; though it is still retained by the Septuagint, and several Latin manuscripts, according to the testimony of Liranus. If we add here, therefore, to the Hebrew text, we must translate it with St. Jerome, thus; *It went forth, going and returning, (Egredicbatur exiens et revertens,)* sometimes repairing to the mountains, where it found carcasses to feed on, and at other times returning not *unto* the ark, but to rest upon the *top* of it. (Estius) (Challoner) --- Or receded farther from it; as the Hebrew may be explained, agreeably to the Vulgate, Septuagint, Syriac, &c. which admit the negation. (Calmet) --- *Till,* as long as the waters covered the earth, not that it returned to the ark afterwards. (Menochius)

VERSE 9

Whole earth, excepting the mountains; so that the dove presently returned. (Haydock)

VERSE 11

Green leaves. The olive tree preserves its verdure and grows even at the bottom of the Red sea, and other seas in the East. (Pliny, Natural History xii. 25.) --- Many other trees and seeds will live for a long time under the waters. (Calmet) --- This tender branch of the olive seems to agree better with the spring than autumn; whence Tirinus infers, that the deluge began and ended in spring.

VERSE 13

Year of Noe's age, who, we may suppose, was born on the first day of the year. So that his 601st year corresponds with the 1657th of the world, B.C. 2343, on which day the deluge ended. Still Noe waited for God's order to leave the ark till the 27th of the ensuing month, when the earth was more perfectly dried. (Haydock) --- *Covering.* Some think that the window was at the top, like a sky-light. (Calmet)

VERSE 17

Increase. Hebrew, "let them increase." This is spoken of the brute creation, the blessing is given to men. (chap. ix.) --- Neither Noe's family, nor any of the animals, had any young in the ark. (Calmet)

VERSE 20

Holocausts, or whole burnt offerings. In which the whole victim was consumed by fire upon God's altar, and no part was reserved for the use of priest or people. (Challoner) --- This is the first time we read of an altar, though Abel had surely made use of one. (Menochius) --- Noe delays not to show his gratitude to God, St. Ambrose. (Worthington)

VERSE 21

Smelled, &c. A figurative expression, denoting that God was pleased with the sacrifices which his servant offered, (Challoner) and in this sense it is expressed in the Chaldee, "God received his offering gratefully." God requires sacrifices of us, to testify his dominion, and not for any advantage he derives from them; but rather to bless us, if we perform our duty with fervor. --- *For the sake of,* or on account of men's sins. They are so prone to evil, that, if I were to punish them as often as they deserve, new deluges might be sent every day. I take pity on their weakness. I will punish the most criminal, but not as I have done, by cursing the earth. These words of God, are by some addressed to Noe, by others to God the Son. Hebrew, "he said to his heart;" Onkelos, "he said in his word;" Septuagint, "he said with reflection." (Calmet) --- Noe was beloved by God, and therefore may be called his heart. To speak to the heart, often means to comfort. (Haydock)

VERSE 22

Seed-time, according to the Targum of Jonathan, is the equinox of September; *harvest,* that of March; winter and summer denote the solstice of December and of June. But the Hebrews probably divided the year into summer and winter; or perhaps they might also admit the season of spring, with the Egyptians and the ancient Greeks, who represented the seasons by the three hours, daughters of Jupiter. (Calmet)

CHAPTER IX

VERSE 1

Blessed, with fecundity. Barrenness was deemed a curse. (Calmet)

VERSE 2

Fear, &c. God confirms the dominion of man over all the animals, though he must exercise it now by compulsion; they will not obey always without reluctance, as they would have done in the state of innocence. (Haydock)

VERSE 3

Meat. The more religious, at least, had hitherto abstained from flesh, being content with herbs, &c.: which had been expressly granted. Now, the salt waters of the deluge had vitiated the earth, its plants were no longer so nutritive. (Menochius) --- God gives leave to eat flesh meat, but with some restriction, that we may still learn to obey. (Worthington)

VERSE 4

With blood. This was a matter of indifference in itself, like the forbidden fruit. But God gave the prohibition, to keep people at a greater distance from imbruing their hands in the blood of others, which nevertheless we know some have drunk! He would also assert his dominion over all things; the blood or life of animals being reserved to be offered in sacrifice to him, instead of the life of man, Leviticus xvii. 11. Blood of brutes is gross and unwholesome. (Menochius) --- The apostles required this law to be observed by the first Christians, that the Jews might not be disgusted: but, after a competent time had been allowed them, the Church thought proper to alter this discipline. (St. Augustine, contra Faust. xxxii. 13.)

VERSE 5

At the hand; a Hebrew idiom. God orders an ox to be stoned, which had slain a man, Exodus xxi. 28. --- *Man,* (hominis) *every man,* (viri) *brother.* By these three terms, God inculcates a horror of bloodshed; because we are all of the same nature, ought to act like generous men, and to consider every individual as a brother, since we spring from the same stock. (Menochius)

VERSE 6

Shed. God had not subjected Cain to this law of retaliation, as he was the first murderer, and the earth was un-peopled. (Haydock) --- Here he declares, that it is just to inflict such a punishment on the offender. (Menochius) --- Judges are hence authorized to punish murderers with death. (Calmet) --- The general law, *thou shalt not kill,* admits of exceptions, and forbids killing by private authority, or out of revenge. (Haydock) --- *The blood of your lives,* may signify the blood on which your life depends; or, according to the Rabbin, it is a prohibition of suicide, which one would think is so contrary to the first law of nature, self-preservation, as to require no prohibition; and yet, to the scandal of philosophers, some have written in its defense! (Haydock)

VERSE 10

Soul...in birds, &c. The covenant of God is made with animals, only in as much as they are subservient to man. (Du Hamel) --- The Egyptians adored most of them; and many oriental nations, and even philosophers, pretended they had intelligent souls, and could speak a rational language, which some of them would have the people believe they could understand. (Calmet) --- This was the case of those great impostors Apollonius of Tyena, Mahomet, &c. (Haydock) --- Moses shows sufficiently that beasts were neither divinities nor rational. (Calmet)

VERSE 13

My rain *bow.* This had been from the beginning; but it was not before appointed for a sign that the earth should no more be destroyed by water. It is styled God's bow, on account of its beauty and grandeur. (Menochius) (Ecclesiasticus xliii. 12.) --- "As the rainbow, which makes its appearance in the clouds, borrows all its effulgence from the sun, so those only who acknowledge the glory of Christ in God's clouds, and do not seek their own glory, will escape destruction in the deluge," St. Augustine, contra Faust. ii. 21.

VERSE 16

Remember; or I shall cause men to reflect, when they see the rainbow, of the horrors of the deluge, and of my gracious promises and covenant.

VERSE 18

Chanaan, who, it seems, is here mentioned to his shame, having first discovered and told his father that Noe was drunk. He was probably but young at the time, being born after the deluge.

VERSE 20

A husbandman. Hebrew, literally "a man of the earth." (Haydock) --- *To till,* perhaps with a plough, which he is said to have invented. (Menochius)

VERSE 21

Drunk. Noe by the judgment of the fathers was not guilty of sin, in being overcome by wine; because he knew not the strength of it. (Challoner) --- *Wine,* Though vines had grown from the beginning, the art of making wine seems not to have been discovered; and hence Noe's fault is much extenuated, and was at most only a venial sin. (Menochius) --- His nakedness prefigured the desolate condition of Christ upon the cross, which was a scandal to the Jews, and foolishness to the Gentiles. But by this folly we are made wise; we are redeemed, and enjoy the name of Christians. Sem and Japheth represent the multitude of believers, Cham and Chanaan the audacity and impudence of all unbelievers. (St. Augustine, contra Faust. xii. 24; City of God xvi. 2; St. Cyprian, ep. 63. ad Cæcil.) (Worthington) --- Like the Manichees, modern heretics are very free in condemning many innocent actions of the Patriarchs. (Haydock)

VERSE 23

Sought we to be so quick-sighted in discovering the faults of any: which we often represent as real, when they are only apparent. (Haydock)

VERSE 25

Cursed be Chanaan. The *curses,* as well as the *blessings,* of the patriarchs were *prophetical* and this in particular is here recorded by Moses, for the children of Israel, who were to possess the land of Chanaan. But why should Chanaan be cursed for his father's fault? The Hebrews answer, that he, being then a boy, was the first that saw his grandfather's nakedness, and told his father Cham of it; and joined with him in laughing at it: which drew upon him, rather than the rest of the children of Cham, this prophetical curse. (Challoner) --- Theodoret, q. 57. The children of Sem executed this sentence, in exterminating many of the Chanaanites under Josue. (Worthington) --- They perished for their own wickedness, which God foresaw, and revealed to Noe. Cham was severely punished by this denunciation of his children's misery. See Milton, xi. 754. xii. 27; Deuteronomy ix. 4. (Haydock)

VERSE 27

Enlarge Japheth. His name signifies latitude or enlargement. (Worthington) --- May *he,* God, according to some; but more probably Japheth, of whom the rest of the sentence speaks. (Haydock) --- This was verified by the extensive dominion of the children of Japheth, both in the islands and on the continent; more particularly, when the Romans subdued the Jews, and posterity of Sem. (Menochius) --- Referring all this to the Church, the Gentiles entered in, upon the refusal of the Jews, though preachers of that nation were the instruments of their conversion. Chanaan, in the mean time, cherished his slavery, and seeks not to obtain the liberty and glory of the sons of God, in which he is a figure of heretics, (Haydock) who serve to make Christians more upon their guard, and by persecuting them, exercise their patience and increase their crown. (Worthington)

VERSE 29

He died, having witnessed the attempt of his children to build the tower of Babel, (we may suppose with disapprobation) and having been concerned in the dispersing of nations. Some imagine he travelled eastward, and founded the empire of China, which is denied by others. (Haydock) --- The fathers conclude that he had no children after the deluge, as the Scripture mentions the world was divided among his three sons and their offspring. Perhaps the fabulous account of Saturn is a perversion of Noe's history, as the three great pagan deities, Jupiter, Neptune, and Pluto, to whom Saturn gave the empire of heaven, seas and hell, may have been intended for the three sons of Noe. The Egyptians have attributed to their Osiris the erecting of altars, cultivating vines, teaching agriculture, &c. for which we have seen Noe was so famous. (Calmet) --- This great and virtuous patriarch had only been dead two years, when the faithful Abraham was born, as it were to succeed him in maintaining the cause of God. (Haydock) ---

The Rabbins assert, that God gave some general laws to Noe, which were necessarily to be observed by all who would obtain salvation: 1. To obey the laws. 2. Not to curse God. 3. Nor admit of any false god, nor of any superstition. 4. Not to marry one's mother, mother-in-law, sister by the same mother, or another person's wife, nor to commit sins against nature. 5. Not to shed blood, that of beasts must be buried. 6. Not to steal, or break one's word. 7. Not to eat the limb of a living creature. Maimonides thinks this last was given to Noe, the rest to Adam. (Calmet)

CHAPTER X
VERSE 1

Japheth. From his being placed first, some conclude that he was the eldest; and perhaps the famed Japetus of the Greeks is the same person. (Du Hamel) --- Sem comes last, though elder than Cham, that the history of the true Church may be more connected. Though it would be a work of great labor to discover what nations sprung from the people here mentioned, yet some are sufficiently obvious; and the learned Bochart has given very plausible applications of the different names to the respective nations, in his *Phaleg.* or sacred Geography. *Gomer* is supposed to be the father of the Cimbri in Germany, from whom the French and English also probably sprung. (Haydock) --- *Magog,* father of the Scythians, &c. (Ezechiel. xxvi.)*Madai* of the Medes, *Javan* of the Ionians in Greece, *Thubal* of the Iberians and Spaniards, *Mosoch* of the Muscovites, *Thiras* of the Thracians.

VERSE 3

The father of the Germans, Thogorma father of the Turks. (Menochius)

VERSE 5

The islands. So the Hebrews called all the remote countries, to which they went by ships to Judea, as Greece, Italy, Spain, &c., (Challoner) whether they were surrounded with water or not. (Jeremias xxv. 22.) (Menochius)

VERSE 9

A stout hunter. Not of beasts, but of men; whom by violence and tyranny he brought under his dominion. And such he was, not only in the opinion of men, but *before the Lord;* that is, in his sight who cannot be deceived. (Challoner) --- The Septuagint call him *a giant;* that is, a *violent* man. According to Josephus, he stirred up men to rebel against the Lord, maintaining that all their happiness must come from themselves, &c., Antiquities i. 4. Thus he broached the first heresy after the deluge. (Worthington) --- He seems to have been the same as Bel, father of Ninus, and the author of idolatry. (Menochius)

VERSE 11

That land, of Sennaar, near the city of Babylon. *Assur,* or Ninus, who founded the Assyrian empire. (Menochius) --- But many understand this of Nemrod, who, in his progress from Babylonia to conquer the world, and oppress the rest of his brethren, *came forth into Assyria,* as if it were written *Assurah;* the *He* signifying motion towards, being often omitted in names of places. See 2 Kings vi. 10. (Bochart.) There he built Ninive, on the Tigris. But the exact situation of this vast city is not even known. (Calmet) --- *And the streets,* &c., which were amazingly extensive, Jonas iii. 3. It may also signify the city *Rohoboth.* (Pagnin.) --- *Chale* perhaps of Halah, 4 Kings xvii. 6, on the banks, or near the source of the river Chaboras.

VERSE 12

Resen, perhaps Larissa, here written without the *La;* as 1 Paralipomenon v. 26. Hala has the preposition, and is written Lahela. (Bochart.) --- *This,* &c. It is doubtful which of these three cities is meant: but as we know that Ninive was remarkable for size and magnificence, we may suppose this is designated. (Calmet) (Menochius)

VERSE 19

To Lesa, or Laisa, to the north, on the Jordan, as Sodom was on the southern extremity of that river. Sidon and Gaza were on the Mediterranean sea, north and south; so that these four cities are like four points, determining the extent of the promised land, which, as it was important for the Israelites to know, Moses descends to these particulars in speaking of the Chanaanites.

VERSE 21

Of Heber. That is, of the nations *beyond* the Euphrates. Hebrews, &c. (Calmet) --- *The elder brother, fratre Japheth majore,* may be rendered as well "Japheth being his elder brother," which, as we have already observed, was probably the case. By mentioning him alone, we may gather that Sem was elder than Cham, who is called the less or younger son. (Haydock) --- The Hebrew may be translated either way. But the Chaldean, Liranus, and many excellent interpreters, make Jepheth the eldest. (Calmet)

VERSE 24

Begot Sale; either his son, or his grandson, by Cainan. See Luke iii. 36, where we shall examine this question; also chap. xi. 12. The copies of the Septuagint still extant, all assert that Cainan was the son of Arphaxad, in all the places where they are mentioned, both in Genesis and Chronicles; and though some endeavor to prove that this is an interpolation, inserted by a later hand, it is certain it was found in the Septuagint in the days of St. Luke, who confirms it by his authority, as all the copies both Greek and Latin, except a very faulty one which belonged to Beza, and is now at Cambridge, testify. Beza was so bold as to expunge the name. But before we allow of this freedom, we must be informed how St. Luke could adopt such an error, being, as he was, under the guidance of the Holy Ghost! See Salien, &c. (Haydock) --- Mariana asserts, that the Hebrew copies have been vitiated.

VERSE 29

Sons of Jectan; though not perhaps all born before the dispersion of nations, which may be said of some others, whom Moses here mentions, that he may not have to interrupt his narration. (Calmet)

CHAPTER XI
VERSE 1

Speech. Probably Hebrew; in which language we have the most ancient book in the world, the work of Moses. This language has been preserved ever since, though with some alterations. Most of the oriental languages are but like dialects from it, as French, Italian, &c. are from Latin. The arguments which are brought to prove that other languages are more ancient, because the names of men, &c. have a proper significance in them as well as in Hebrew, do not invalidate the right of the latter. The most respectable authors have, therefore, always declared for it (Haydock)

VERSE 2

The East: Armenia, which lies to the eastward of Babylonia, whither they directed their course in quest of provisions for themselves and cattle, being now grown pretty numerous. (Menochius)

VERSE 3

Each one: not that every individual joined in this undertaking, considered, at least, as a rash and presumptuous attempt to save themselves from a second deluge. Some might innocently give in to it, meaning only to leave a monument to their common origin and friendship, before they separated into distant countries. *Slime:* literally bitumen. (Haydock) --- The Hebrew, *chomer,* means also slime, or mortar. Stone is very scarce in that country, but the earth is fat, and very proper to make brick; it also abounds in naphtha, bitumen, &c.: hence the ancients notice the brick walls of Babylon. (Calmet)

VERSE 4

Famous before; Hebrew *lest,* &c.; as if they intended to prevent that event. (Haydock) --- Their motive appears to have been pride, which raised the indignation of God. Nemrod, the chief instigator, might have designed the tower for a retreat, whence he might sally out and maintain his tyranny. (Menochius)

VERSE 6

Indeed. This seems to be spoken ironically; though the effects of weak mortals, *the sons of Adam,* when pursued with vigor and unanimity, will produce great effects. These builders had conceived an idea of raising the tower as high as possible, hyperbolically, to touch heaven. (Haydock)

VERSE 7

Come ye, &c. As men seemed bent on taking heaven by storm, like the ancient giants, God turns their expressions, as it were, against themselves, and shows them an example of humility, *let us go down.* He acts the part of a judge, and therefore will examine all with the utmost diligence, as he denotes by these expressions; being really incapable of moving from place to place, on account of his immensity. (Haydock) --- He seems nearer to men, by the effects or punishments which he inflicted. The address which he here makes is directed, not to the angels, but to the other co-equal powers of the Blessed Trinity. (Menochius)

VERSE 9

Babel, that is, *confusion.* This is one of the greatest miracles recorded in the Old Testament; men forgot, in a moment, the language which they had hitherto spoken, and found themselves enabled to speak another, known only to a few of the same family (Calmet); for we must not suppose that there were as many new languages as there were men at Babel. (Menochius) --- The precise number of languages which were then heard, cannot be determined. The learned commonly acknowledge the Hebrew, Greek, Latin, Teutonic, Sclavonian, Tartarian, and Chinese languages, to be original. The rest are only dialects from these. English is chiefly taken from the Teutonic, (Calmet) with many words borrowed from the Greek and other languages. (Haydock)

VERSE 12

Sale, or Cainan. See Chap. x. 24; Chronicles i. 18, in the Septuagint. (Haydock)

VERSE 20

Sarug: in whose days St. Epiphanius places the origin of idolatry; but Eusebius (Præp. i. v. & 9.) thinks it began in Egypt, among the posterity of Cham. (Calmet)

VERSE 27

Abram, the youngest of the three, being born only in the 130th year of Thare, ver. 32, and chap. xii. 4. He is placed first, on account of his superior dignity in the church of God, in like manner as Sem, Moses, &c. In his youth, he is supposed to have followed the idolatrous worship of his fathers. (St. Augustine, City of God x. chap. ultra[last chap.]; Genebrard, A.M. 1949 [in the year of the world 1949].) (Calmet) --- But being soon enlightened by God, he becomes a glorious witness of the truth, and, according to many, is preserved miraculously, when thrown into the fire *by the Chaldees,* ver. 31. (Haydock)

VERSE 29

Jescha, whom many confound with Sarai, as if both Nacher and Abram had married the daughters of their brother Aran. But why then does Moses mention Sarai before, and then call her Jescha in the same verse? It seems as if he intended to designate two different women. (Haydock) --- In effect, Abram himself says, Sarai was truly his *sister, born of the same father,* chap. xii. 13. See chap. xx. 12, where we shall give the reasons that seem to prove that she was the daughter of Thare, and not Aran. (Calmet) --- Jescha does not accompany her grandfather, preferring, perhaps, to stay with Nachor, or to marry in her own country; if she were not already dead when Thare departed from *Ur,* a city *of the Chaldees.*(Haydock) --- This city is probably Ura, in Mesopotamia, not far from Nisibis, which the Scripture often mentions is a part of Chaldea. (Acts. vii. 2, &c.) (Calmet) --- It is not, however certain that the rest of Thare's family remained behind; if they did, they removed soon after into the country about Haran, or Charræ, on the Charboras. (chap. xxix. 4; Josephus, Antiquities 1. 6.) (Haydock)

CHAPTER XII

VERSE 1

Said: not after his father's death, but before he left Ur; (Menochius) unless, perhaps, Abram received a second admonition at Haran, which, from his dwelling there with his father, &c., is styled his country. He leaves his *kindred,* Nachor and his other relations, except Sarai and Lot, who go with him unto Chanaan; and even his *own house,* or many of his domestics and effects, and full of faith, goes in quest of an unknown habitation, Hebrews xi. 8. (Haydock) --- St. Stephen clearly distinguishes these two calls of Abram. From the second, the 430 years of sojournment, mentioned Galatians iii; Exodus xii, must be dated. (Calmet) --- This is the third grand epoch of the world, about 2083, when God chooses one family to maintain the one faith, which he had all along supported. See Worthington &c.

VERSE 3

In thee, &c., or in the Messias, who will be one of thy descendants, and the source of all the blessings to be conferred on any of the human race, Galatians iii. 16. Many of the foregoing promises regarded a future world, and Abram was by no means incredulous, when he found himself afflicted here below, as if God had forgot his promises. (Calmet) --- He was truly blessed, in knowing how to live poor in spirit, even amid riches and honors; faithful in all tribulations and trials; *following God* in all things, ver. 1.

VERSE 5

Gotten, (fecerant): made or acquired, either by birth or purchase, &c. (Menochius)

VERSE 6

Sichem. At the foot of Mt. Garizim, where Abram offered his first sacrifice in the land, Deuteronomy xi. 30. (Kennicott) --- *Noble;* on account of the many tall and shady oaks, whence the Septuagint have the high oak. Hebrew *Elon more,* the plain of Moreh, or of extension, because God showed Abram from this place, situated about the middle of the promised land, what countries he would give to him in his posterity, after having exterminated the Chanaanites, who then occupied the land as their own. The mentioning of these idolatrous nations here, gives us reason to admire the faith and constancy of Abram, who neither doubted of the fulfilling of this promise, nor hesitated to adore the true God publicly, ver. 7. Hence there is no reason for accounting this an interpolation. (Haydock)

VERSE 8

Bethel, as it was called in the days of Moses, being the ancient Luza, chap. 28. *On the west,* Hebrew, towards the sea or Mediterranean, which lay west of Palestine. *Bethel* signifies *the house of God,* being honored with two altars. (Haydock)

VERSE 9

Proceeding to the south, Hebrew: means also *the desert,* as the Septuagint generally translate *negeb:* other interpreters agree with the Vulgate. (Calmet)

VERSE 10

Down into Egypt, which lies lower than Judea: here the famine did not rage. God would not allow him to go back to his friends. (Menochius)

VERSE 11

Beautiful: having yet had no children, though she must have been 65 years old. Abram acts with prudence, and does not tempt God: if he had made known that the woman was his wife, he would have exposed his life to imminent danger, amid a cruel and lascivious people; and being convinced of the chastity of Sarai, he did not, in the least, apprehend that she would consent to any violation of her conjugal engagements. He did not, therefore, expose her virtue as the Manichees pretended. (St. Augustine, contra Faust. xxii. 33; City of God xvi. 19.) (Haydock; Calmet) --- The event proved the justice of Abram's suspicions, and God's interference showed that he was not displeased with his concealing part of the truth. Who can be so simple as to suppose, that we are bound to explain all our concerns to a foe? Do not we every day act with the like caution as Abram did, when we have reason to fear danger? Do not we wish, when fleeing from an enemy's country, that he should conclude we were taking a walk of pleasure? (Haydock)

VERSE 13

My sister. This was no lie; because she was his niece, being daughter to his brother Aran, and therefore, in the style of the Hebrews, she might truly be called his *sister;* as Lot is called Abraham's *brother.*(Genesis xiv. 14.) See Genesis xx. 12. (Challoner) --- Others say, Sarai was the half-sister of Abraham, by another mother. (Haydock)

VERSE 15

Pharao: The usual title of the kings of Egypt, in Ezechiel's time, Ezechiel xxxii. 2. Couriers are often too ready to flatter the passions of the prince: these are punished along with Pharao (ver. 17); whence we may conclude, that they concurred with him, to take Sarai against her will.

VERSE 16

Well. Perhaps they made him some presents to gain his favor; (Menochius) or, at least, they suffered him to remain quietly among them.

VERSE 17

Scourged Pharao with unusual pains, sterility, &c. that he might easily perceive that his taking Sarai was displeasing to God. (Haydock) --- He did not intend to commit adultery indeed, but his conduct was tyrannical and oppressive to the *stranger,* whom God protects, Psalm 44. (Menochius)

VERSE 20

Led him away: perhaps without allowing him time to vindicate his conduct, and with a degree of contumely, to show the king's displeasure; who durst not, however, injure Abraham in his effects, nor suffer any of his subjects to hurt him. The holy patriarch received his wife untouched, and departed with joy. (Haydock)

CHAPTER XIII
VERSE 2

Rich in possession. Hebrew may be "heavy laden with cattle, gold," &c. (Menochius)

VERSE 6

To bear or feed their flocks, as well as those of the Chanaanites. (Calmet)

VERSE 8

Abram therefore, for fear of raising a quarrel with the Pherezites also, who might complain that these strangers were eating up what they had before taken possession of, suggests to his nephew the propriety of their taking different courses. Being the older, he divides, and the younger chooses, according to an ancient and laudable custom. (St. Augustine, City of God xvi. 20.)

VERSE 11

From the east of Pentapolis to Sodom, (Menochius) or to the east of the place where Abram was, as Onkelos has it. The Hebrew may signify either. (Grotius.)

VERSE 13

Sinners before, &c. That is, truly, without restraint or disguise. Lot might not have been acquainted with their dissolute morals, when he made this choice; in which however he consulted only his senses, and looked for temporal advantages, which ended in sorrow. This God permitted for a warning to us; and to restrain the Sodomites, by the example of Lot's justice, contrasted with the abominable lives. (Haydock) --- Ezechiel xvi. 49, explains the causes of their wickedness.

VERSE 15

And to: This is by way of explanation to the former words: (Haydock) for Abram never possessed a foot of this land by inheritance, Acts viii. 5. Even his posterity never enjoyed it, at least, for any long time. St. Augustine gives the reason; because the promise was conditional, and the Jews did not fulfill their part by obedience and fidelity. (q. 3. in Gen.) It is better, however, to understand these promises of another land, which the people, who imitate the faith of Abram, shall enjoy in the world to come. (Calmet) (Romans iv. 16.)

VERSE 16

As the dust, an hyperbole, to express a very numerous offspring, which is more exact, if we take in the spiritual children of Abram. (Menochius)

VERSE 17

Through. Lot has chosen a part, I give the whole to thee. Thou mayest take possession of it, and go wherever thou hast a mind. (Calmet)

VERSE 18

Vale, or *grove of oaks,* where there was a famous one which was called the oak of Mambre, either from the neighboring city, or from a man of that name, chap. xiv. 13. (Menochius) --- Hebron was on the hill above. (Calmet)

VERSE 20

South. With respect to Judea, which the sacred writers have always in view.

CHAPTER XIV

VERSE 1

Sennaar, or Babylon. --- *Pontus,* Hebrew: Ellasar, perhaps Thalassar, as Jonathan writes, not far from Eden. --- *Elamites,* or Persians. --- *Nations* in Galilee, east of the Jordan, whither the conquered kings directed their course. Josue xii. 23, mentions the king of the nations (foreigners) at Galgal. (Calmet)

VERSE 3

Now, in the days of Moses. --- *Salt sea;* called also the vale of salts, and the dead sea.

VERSE 4

Served. Thus Noe's prediction began to be fulfilled, as Elam was the eldest son of Sem, to whose posterity Chanaan should be slaves, chap. ix. 26.

VERSE 5

Raphaim, Zuzim, and *Emim,* were all of the gigantic race, robbers, like the Arabs. (Du Hamel) --- These dwelt in the land of Basan, or of giants, Deuteronomy iii. 13.

VERSE 6

Chorreans, or Horreans, who dwelt in one part of that extensive range of mountains, which took their name from Seir; perhaps about mount Hor, where Aaron died. (Calmet) --- These also were auxiliaries of the five kings, and hence experienced the fury of the four confederates; who cut off all their opponents, before they made their grand attack upon Sodom. (Haydock)

VERSE 7

Misphat, or of judgment and contradiction, because there the Hebrews contended with Moses and Aaron: it was afterwards called Cadez, Numbers xx. 11. --- *Amalecites,* that is which they afterwards possessed; for as yet Amelec was unborn, chap. xxxvi. 16. (Menochius) --- *Amorrheans,* to the west of Sodom. (Calmet)

VERSE 10

Of slime. Bituminis. This was a kind of pitch, which served for mortar in the building of Babel, Genesis xi. 3, and was used by Noe in pitching the ark. (Challoner) --- Moses does not make this remark without reason. This bitumen would easily take fire, and contribute to the conflagration of Sodom. (Calmet) ---*Overthrown,* not all slain, for the king of Sodom escaped, ver. 17.

VERSE 13

The Hebrew, or traveler who came from beyond the Euphrates, (Calmet) or who dwelt beyond the Jordan, with reference to the five kings. (Diodorus)

VERSE 14

Servants, fit for war. Hence we may form some judgment of the power and dignity of Abram, who was considered as a great prince in that country, chap. xxiii. 6. He was assisted by Mambre, Escol, and Aner, with all the forces they could raise on such a short warning; and coming upon the four kings unawares, in four divisions, easily discomfits them, while they were busy plundering the cities, and pursues them *to Dan;* which is either the city that went by that name afterwards, or more probably one of the sources of the Jordan, (Haydock) which the people of the country call *Medan.* Neither did he suffer them to repose, before he had retaken all the plunder at *Hoba,* or Abila, north of the road leading to Damascus. (Calmet)

VERSE 18

Melchisedech was not Sem for his genealogy is given in Scripture. (Hebrew xii. 6.); nor God the Son, for they are compared together; nor the Holy Ghost, as some have asserted; but a virtuous Gentile who adored the true God, and was *king of Salem,* or Jerusalem, and *Priest* of an order different from that of Aaron, offering in sacrifice *bread and wine,* a figure of Christ's sacrifice in the Mass; as the fathers constantly affirm. (Haydock) --- See Pererius. St. Jerome, ep. ad Evagrium, says, "Melchisedech offered not bloody victims, but dedicated the sacrament of Christ in bread and wine...a pure sacrifice." See St. Cyprian ep. 63, ad Cæcil.; St. Augustine, City of God xvi. 22, &c. Many Protestants confess, that this renowned prince of Chanaan, was also a priest; but they will not allow that his sacrifice consisted of bread and wine. In what then? for a true priest must offer some real sacrifice. If *Christ,* therefore, be *a priest for ever according to the order of Melchisedech,* whose sacrifice was not bloody, as those of Aaron were, what other sacrifice does he now offer, but that of his own body and blood in the holy Mass, by the ministry of his priests *for he was the priest:* this is plainly referred to *bringing forth,* &c., which shows that word to be sacrificial, as in Judges vi. 18. The Hebrew may be ambiguous. But all know that *vau* means *for* as well as *and.* Thus the English Bible had it, 1552, "for he was the priest." (Worthington) --- If Josephus take notice only of Melchisedech, offering Abram and his men corporal refreshment, we need not wonder; he was a Jewish priest, to whom the order of Melchisedech might not be agreeable. It is not indeed improbable, but Abram might partake of the meat, which had been offered in thanksgiving by Melchisedech; and in this sense his words are true. But there would be no need of observing, that he was a priest on this account; as this was a piece of civility expected from princes on similar occasions. (Deuteronomy xxiii. 4; 2 Kings xvii. 27.) (Haydock)

VERSE 19

Blessed him, as his inferior, and received tithes of him, Hebrews iv. 7. This shows the antiquity of the practice of supporting God's priests by tithes.

VERSE 21

The persons (*animas*), the souls subject to my dominion. (Haydock)

I lift up. This is the posture of one swearing solemnly, by which we testify our belief, that God dwells in the heavens, and governs the world. (Calmet)

Woof-thread. The first word is added by way of explanation. Abram declares he will not receive the smallest present for himself.

Their shares, due to them on account of the danger to which they had exposed themselves. The king of Sodom could not but accept these conditions with gratitude. In a just war, whatever is taken by the enemy cannot be reclaimed by the original proprietor, if it be retaken. (Grotius, iii. 6, de Jure.)

CHAPTER XV
VERSE 1

Fear not. He might naturally be under some apprehensions, lest the four kings should attempt to be revenged upon him. --- *Reward,* since thou hast so generously despised earthly riches. (Haydock) --- Abram was not asleep, but saw a vision of exterior objects, ver. 5.

VERSE 2

I shall go. To what purpose should I heap up riches, since I have no son to inherit them? Abram knew that God had promised him a numerous posterity; but he was not apprized how this was to be verified, and whether he was to adopt some other for his son and heir. Therefore, he asks modestly, how he out to understand the promise. --- *And the son,* &c. Hebrew is differently rendered, "and the steward of my house, this Eliezer of Damascus." We know not whether Eliezer or Damascus be the proper name. The Septuagint have "the son of Mesech, my handmaid, this Eliezer of Damascus." Most people suppose, that Damascus was the son of Eliezer, the steward. The sentence is left unfinished, and must be supplied from the following verse, *shall be my heir.* The son of the steward, *filius procurationis,* may mean the steward himself, as the son of perdition denotes the person lost. (Calmet)

VERSE 6

Reputed by God, who cannot judge wrong; so that Abram increased in justice by this act of faith, believing that his wife, now advanced in years, would have a child; from whom others should spring, more numerous than the stars of heaven. (Haydock) --- This faith was accompanied and followed by many other acts of virtue, St. James ii. 22. (Worthington)

VERSE 8

Whereby, &c. Thus the blessed Virgin asked, how shall this be done? Luke i. 34, without the smallest degree of unbelief. Abram wished to know, by what signs he should be declared the lawful owner of the land. (Haydock)

VERSE 9

Three years, when these animals have obtained a perfect age.

VERSE 12

A deep sleep, or ecstasy, like that of Adam, chap. ii. 21, wherein God revealed to him the oppression of his posterity in Egypt, which filled him with such *horror* (Menochius) as we experience when something frightful comes upon us suddenly in the dark. This *darkness* represents the dismal situation of Joseph, confined in a dungeon; and of the Hebrews condemned to hard labor, in making bricks, and obliged to hide their male children, for fear of their being discovered, and slain. Before these unhappy days commenced, the posterity of

Abram were exposed to great oppression among the Chanaanites, nor could they in any sense be said to possess the land of promise, for above 400 years after this prophetic sleep. (Haydock)

VERSE 13

Strangers, and under bondage, &c. This prediction may be dated from the persecution of Isaac by Ismael, in the year 2112, till the Jews left Egypt, 2513. In Exodus xii and St. Paul, 430 years are mentioned; but they probably began when Abram went first into Egypt, 2084. Nicholas Abram and Tournemine say, the Hebrews remained in Egypt full 430 years from the captivity of Joseph; and reject the addition of the Septuagint which adds, "they and their fathers dwelt in Egypt, and in Chanaan." On these points, we may expect to find chronologists at variance.

VERSE 14

Judge and punish the Egyptians, overwhelming them in the Red sea, &c. (Haydock)

VERSE 16

Fourth, &c. after the 400 years are finished; during which period of time, God was pleased to bear with those wicked nations; whose iniquity chiefly consisted in idolatry, oppression of the poor and strangers, forbidden marriages of kindred, and abominable lusts. (Leviticus xviii; Deuteronomy vi. and xii.) (Menochius)

VERSE 17

A lamp, or symbol of the Divinity, passing, as Abram also did, between the divided beasts, to ratify the covenant. See Jeremias xxxiv. 18.

VERSE 18

Of Egypt, a branch of the Nile, not far from Pelusium. This was to be the southern limit, and the Euphrates the northern; the two other boundaries are given, Numbers xxxiv. --- Perhaps Solomon's empire extended so far. At least, the Jews would have enjoyed these territories, if they had been faithful. (Menochius)

VERSE 19

Cineans, in Arabia, of which nation was Jethro. They were permitted to dwell in the tribe of Juda, and served the Hebrews. --- *Cenezites,* who probably inhabited the mountains of Juda. --- *Cedmonites,* or*eastern* people, as their name shows. Cadmus was of this nation, of the race of the Heveans, dwelling in the environs of mount Hermon, whence his wife was called Hermione. He was, perhaps, one of those who fled at the approach of Josue; and was said to have sowed dragons' teeth, to people his city of Thebes in Beotia, from an allusion to the name of the Hevites, which signifies serpents. (Calmet) --- The eleven nations here mentioned were not all subdued; on account of the sins of the Hebrews. (Menochius)

CHAPTER XVI
VERSE 2

May have. Hebrew, "may be built up," a metaphorical expression: so God is said to have built up houses for the Egyptian midwives, Exodus i. 21. (Menochius)

VERSE 3

Ten years after she was 65; which shows that she might reasonably conclude she would now have no children herself; and as she knew God had promised Abram a son, she thought he might follow the custom of those times, and have him by a second wife. Abram showed no eagerness on this matter, but only yielded to his wife's petition, *deprecanti,* being well aware of the inconveniences of polygamy, which Sarai had soon reason to observe. This is the first time we read of polygamy since the deluge; but it is not mentioned as anything singular or unlawful. This was a matter in which God could dispense; but it was never left to the disposal of any man. Hence, when Luther and his associates ventured to dispense with the Landgrave of Hesse, to keep two wives at once, he required him to keep it a secret, being ashamed of his own conduct. He still maintained it was a thing indifferent, even in the law of grace, though Christ has so expressly condemned it. See præp 62, 65. The practice, so common of late in this country, of marrying again after a bill of divorce has been passed, is no less contrary to the Catholic doctrine, which allows only a separation of the parties from bed and board, in cases of adultery; but never of a second marriage, while both the parties are living. (1 Corinthians vii.; St. Augustine de Adult. Conj. i., City of God xvi. 25, 38; and other fathers.) (Haydock) --- It was never lawful for one woman to have two husbands. (Worthington) --- *To wife.* Plurality of wives, though contrary to the primitive institution of marriage, Genesis ii. 24, was by Divine dispensation allowed to the patriarchs; which allowance seems to have continued during the time of the law of Moses. But Christ our Lord reduced marriage to its primitive institution, St. Matthew xix.

VERSE 5

Despiseth. Few bear prosperity in a proper manner! --- *And thee.* Sarai things it is the duty of her husband to restrain the insolence of Agar. She commits her cause to God, and does not seek revenge. (Menochius)

VERSE 6

Afflicted her, as she now resented even a moderate correction. (Haydock)

VERSE 7

In the desert; omitted in Hebrew being a repetition of *in the wilderness.* (Calmet)

VERSE 9

Humble thyself. The angel, in God's name, does not blame Sarai; but gives Agar to understand that the fault was wholly on her side. (Haydock)

VERSE 11

Ismael, means "God hath heard" the groans and distress of Agar. (Calmet)

VERSE 12

Wild. Hebrew: like a *wild ass,* not to be tamed or subdued. The Saracens or Arabs, have almost all along maintained their independence. --- *Over against,* ready to fight, without any dread of any one. (Calmet)

VERSE 13

Thou the God. She had imagined before that she was talking to some man; but perceiving, at parting, that it was some superior being, she invoked him thus. ---*The hinder parts,* as Moses did afterwards, Exodus xxxiii, to let us know, that we cannot fully comprehend the nature of an angel, much less of God. Hebrew may be: "what! have I seen (do I live) after He has seen me." The Hebrews generally supposed, that death would presently overtake the person who had seen the Lord or his angel. (Judges vi. 22; Exodus xxxii. 20.) (Calmet)

VERSE 15

Agar being returned home, and having obtained pardon. --- *Ismael,* as the angel had foretold; an honor shown to very few; such as Isaac, Solomon, Jesus, &c. (Haydock)

CHAPTER XVII
VERSE 1

Walk, &c. by assiduous meditation and advancement in virtue. This apparition was to inform Abram that the promised seed should be born of Sarai. (Haydock)

VERSE 4

I am unchangeable, and faithful to my promises, the only God. (Du Hamel) --- *Nations.* Jews, Saracens or Arabs, Idumeans, and, by faith, of all nations who shall believe in Christ, the King of kings. (Calmet) --- The true Church will never then be reduced to a few unknown believers, as the Donatists and Protestants assert. (Worthington)

VERSE 5

Abraham. Abram, in the Hebrew, signifies *a high father;* but Abraham, the *father of the multitude: Sarai* signifies *my Lady,* but *Sara* absolutely *Lady.*(Challoner) --- God thus receives them, as it were, into his own family. (Calmet)

VERSE 7

Perpetual; that shall last as long as they remain obedient. (Menochius) (ver. 9.)

VERSE 11

You shall, either by yourselves, or by the ministry of others, with respect to infants. That part of the body was chosen, because the effects of sin first appeared there; and because a part of the Hebrews' creed was, that Christ should be born of the family of Abraham. --- *A sign* that Abraham had agreed to the covenant with God, and to be a memorial of his faith and justice, Romans iv. 2; to distinguish also the faithful from infidels; to purge away original sin in male children, eight days old; and to be a figure of baptism. (Menochius) (Tirinus) --- God always appoints some sign of his covenants, as Jesus Christ instituted the holy sacrament of his body and blood, under exterior appearances, to assure us of his new alliance with Christians. (Calmet) --- The sacraments of the old law caused grace, only by means of faith in the Redeemer, of which they were signs. (St. Augustine, de Nupt. ii. chap. ultra) In this sense, the holy fathers assert, that circumcision remitted original sin to those who could receive it; though some think, it was only a bare sign or distinctive mark of the Jews. (Calmet) --- It is far beneath our baptism, which is more easy, general and efficacious; as the Christian sacraments are not like those of Moses, *weak and needy elements.* (Galatians iv. 9; St. Augustine ep. 158, ad Jan.; Psalm 73, &c.) (Worthington)

VERSE 12

Days, when he will be able to bear the pain without danger. This might be deferred for a just reason, as it was in the desert, Josue v. 6. In this case people might be saved, as younger children and all females might, by the application of the remedies used in the law of nature, sacrifice, the faith of parents, &c. (Menochius) --- *Of your stock,* and, being arrived at years of discretion, is desirous of enjoying your privileges. Some think, that slaves had no choice left; but servants, and people who had a mind to live in the country, were not bound to submit to this rite against their will. It is even more probable, that none were under this obligation, except Abraham and his posterity by Isaac. His other children adopted it in part, but not with the exactitude of the Jews. (Calmet)

VERSE 14

Circumcised. Septuagint adds, "on the eighth day," with the Samaritan and many Latin copies. (Calmet) --- *Destroyed,* &c. lose the privileges of the Hebrews, or be put to death, when he grows up and does not supply this defect. St. Augustine reading on the eighth day, concluded that as a child of that age, could not, with reason, be put to death for an offense, in which he could have no share, the destruction here threatened is that of the soul, for transgression, in Adam, the original covenant, and dying in that state unclean, must be excluded from heaven, as people are now who die un-baptized. This difficult passage may, however, be explained as if the threat regarded the negligent parents. "He who shall not circumcise shall be destroyed." Syriac, or, as the Hebrew may be rendered, "the male that doth not," &c.; in which case, he becomes guilty of a transgression, when he is arrived at the years sufficient to understand his duty, and does not fulfill it. (Worthington)

VERSE 15

Sara, princess of all the nations of the faithful, not simply of one family. (Menochius)

VERSE 16

Bless, and enable her to have *a son,* who shall also have many children. --- *Whom.* This is referred to Sara, in Hebrew and Chaldean; but to Isaac, in the Syriac. The blessing, at any rate, reverts to the mother; who was a figure of the blessed Virgin, and of the Church; both persecuted with their children; both, in the end, triumphant. (Galatians iv. 23.) (Calmet)

VERSE 17

Laughed for joy and admiration at such unexpected news. "He rejoiced," says the Chaldean, the faith of Abraham is never called into question. (Romans iv. 19.)

VERSE 18

Before thee, under thy protection, and in a virtuous manner. (Menochius) --- He seems to be satisfied, though God should not bless him with any more children, provided this one may live worthy of God. (Haydock)

VERSE 19

Isaac, "laughter," alluding to the exultation of Abraham, more than to the laughter of Sara, which deserved some reprehension, chap. xxi. 6.

Verse 20

Nation of Arabs, who are still divided into twelve tribes. See chap. xxv. 13. (Calmet)

VERSE 23

His house. All were kept in such good order by their master, that none was found unwilling to submit, if indeed it was left to their choice. (Haydock) --- Abraham loses no time in complying with God's commands. (Menochius)

VERSE 25

Full thirteen, or beginning his fourteenth year, at which age the Arabs and Mahometans still generally circumcise; but without any order from God. (Calmet)

CHAPTER XVIII
VERSE 1

Sitting, &c., that he might lose no opportunity of exercising hospitality.

VERSE 2

Men in outward appearance, but angels indeed. (Hebrews xiii. 2; St. Augustine, City of God xvi. chap. 29.) Some have supposed, that one of them was the Son of God, whom Abraham adored, and who bears throughout the chief authority. *Tres vidit et unum adoravit.* He saw three and adored one, as we read in the Church office. In the former supposition, which is generally adopted, this adoration was only a civil ceremony, if Abraham considered them as mere men; or it might be mixed with a degree of religious, though inferior veneration, if he imagined they were angels; or in fine, he adored God in his representatives. (Haydock)

VERSE 4

Wash ye, or let your feet be washed by me, or by my servants, *laventur.*(Menochius)

VERSE 5

Therefore, Providence has directed you hither. Abraham promises but little, and gives much, in the true spirit of generous hospitality. (Calmet)

VERSE 6

Measures, or one epha; that is, three pecks and three pints, English corn measure. --- *Flour,* of the finest quality, *similæ.* --- *Hearth,* as being soonest ready.

VERSE 7

Himself. These rich and truly noble people, do not esteem it beneath them to wait on strangers. They provide abundance, but no dainties. (Haydock)

VERSE 9

Eaten apparently. Tobias xii. 19, or perhaps they consumed the food, as fire may be said to eat. (St. Justin Martyr's Dialogue with Trypho the Jew.)

VERSE 10

Time, or season of the year ensuing, if I be alive; which he says after the manner of men, as he had assumed also the human form. (Haydock)

VERSE 12

Laughed, as if the promise were incredible. --- *My lord,* or husband, which title of respect, 1 Peter iii. 6, commends. (Du Hamel)

VERSE 13

Indeed. This was the import of Sara's words. By thus revealing what was secretly done in the tent, he showed himself to be more than man.

VERSE 14

Hard. So Gabriel says to the blessed Virgin: *there is nothing impossible to God,* Luke i. 37.

VERSE 15

Afraid; which does not entirely clear her of sin: for though she might innocently laugh, if she thought the person who spoke was only a man, yet she ought not to have told an untruth; and if she reflected, that he had disclosed what she supposed no one knew, and thereby manifested his superiority over man, her denial was still more inexcusable. But she was taken, as it were, by surprise; and therefore the Lord reproves her very gently. (Haydock)

VERSE 21

I will go down, &c. The Lord here accommodates his discourse to the way of speaking and acting amongst men: for he knoweth all things, and needeth not to go anywhere for information. --- Note here, that two of the three angels went away immediately for Sodom; whilst the third, who represented the Lord, remained with Abraham.

VERSE 25

With the wicked. God frequently suffers the just to be here the most afflicted; designing to reward them abundantly hereafter. But this was not so common in the days of Abraham and Job. (Calmet)

VERSE 32

Ten. Abraham's chief solicitude was for Lot; though, out of modesty, he does not mention him; trusting, however, in the divine goodness the he would be preserved, unless he had forfeited his justice, he proceeds no farther. God thus challenges Jerusalem to produce *one virtuous man,* and the city shall be saved for his sake, Jeremias v. 1. (Haydock)

CHAPTER XIX
VERSE 1

Ground. Thus showing himself a true relation and imitator of Abraham.

VERSE 2

My lords. He took them to be men. --- *No.* They refuse at first, that he may have the merit of pressing them to accept the invitation. (Haydock)

VERSE 4

Together. The whole city was corrupt; even the children were taught iniquity, as soon as they came to the years of discretion. (Menochius)

VERSE 5

Know them. They boldly proclaim their infamous design.

VERSE 7

This evil, so contrary to the rights of hospitality, and the law of nature.

VERSE 8

Known man. They were neglected, while men were inflamed with desires of each other. See Romans i. (Haydock) --- *Abuse.* Lot tries by every means to divert them from their purpose; being well assured, that they would have nothing to do with his daughters, who were promised to some of the inhabitants. He endeavors to gain time, hoping perhaps that his guests would escape by some back way, while he is talking to the people. (Haydock) ---Some allow that, under so great a perturbation of mind, he consented to an action which could never be allowed, though it was a less evil. (Menochius)

VERSE 9

Thither; from whence thou camest, or into the house. Dost thou pretend to tell us what is wrong? We will treat thee more shamefully. (Menochius) While they are beginning to offer violence.

VERSE 10

Behold, &c. the angels not only secure Lot, but strike the whole people with blindness, so that they could neither find Lot's door nor their own homes. Indeed, if they had been able to get back into their own houses, it would have been but a small consolation to them; since in a few minutes, the whole city was buried in sulfur and flame, Wisdom xix. 16.

VERSE 14

Sons-in-law. Perhaps they also were among the crowd, (ver. 4) and therefore deserved to be abandoned to their incredulity; though, if they would have consented to follow Lot, the angels would have saved them for his sake. --- *In jest.* So little did they suffer God's judgments to disturb them!

VERSE 16

He lingered, entreating the Lord to save the city; and loath, perhaps to lose all his property, for the sake of which he had chosen that abode. --- *Spared him,* and his wife and two daughters, for his sake. These four were all that were even tolerably just: for we find them all soon giving signs of their weakness, and of the danger to which even the best are exposed by evil communications. (Haydock)

VERSE 17

Look not back. Flee with all expedition; let no marks of pity for the wretched Sodomites, nor of sorrow for the loose of your property, be seen.

VERSE 18

My lord, addressing himself to the angel, who led him and his wife. (Menochius)

VERSE 19

The mountain above Segor. He is faint-hearted, and does not comply with readiness and exactitude; though, when he had obtained leave to remain in Segor, he still fears, and flees to the mountain, ver. 30, (Haydock) on the south-east of the dead sea. (Calmet)

VERSE 22

Segor. That is, *a little one.* (Challoner) --- In allusion to Lot's words, ver. 20. As it was small, fewer sinners would of course be contained in it. God had resolved to spare it, and therefore inspired Lot to pray for its preservation. (Menochius) --- Hence we may learn, how great a treasure and safeguard the just man is. (Haydock)

VERSE 23

Risen. It was morning when he left Sodom; (ver. 15.) so this city must not have been very distant. It was before called Bala, or *swallowed up,* and afterwards Salissa. Theodoret supposes it was destroyed as soon as Lot had left it; and it seems Lot's daughters thought so, since they concluded all men, except their father, had perished.

VERSE 24

The Lord rained...from the Lord, in a miraculous manner. Sodom and the other cities did not perish by earthquakes and other natural causes only, but by the divine wrath exerting itself in a visible manner. Here is an insinuation of a plurality of persons in God, as the C [Council] of Sirmich declares, c.[canon?] 14. --- *And Gomorrha,* and the other towns which were not so large, nor perhaps so infamous. ---*Brimstone and fire;* to denote the bad odor and violence of their disorders. (Menochius)

VERSE 25

All the inhabitants, both the body and soul, Jude ver. 7: even the infants would probably die in original sin, as their parents were unbelievers, and careless of applying the proper remedies. (Haydock) --- The women imitated the men in pride and dissolute morals, so that all deserved to perish. (Menochius) --- *All things;* so that even now the environs are barren, and the lake dark and smoking. (Tirinus)

VERSE 26

And his wife. As a standing memorial to the servants of God to proceed in virtue, and not to look back to vice or its allurements. (Challoner) --- *His,* Lot's *wife.* The two last verses might be within a parenthesis. --- *Remember Lot's wife,* our Savior admonishes us. Having begun a good work, let us not leave it imperfect, and lose our reward. (Luke xvii; Matthew xxiv) --- *A statue of durable metallic salt,* petrified as it were, to be an eternal monument of *an incredulous soul,* Wisdom x. 7. Some say it still exists. (Haydock) --- God may have inflicted this temporal punishment on her, and saved her soul. (Menochius) --- She looked back, as if she distrusted the words of the angel; but her fault was venial. (Tirinus)

VERSE 29

Lot. Even he owed his safety to the merits of Abraham.

VERSE 31

No man. If this had been true, Lot might have had children by them, without any fault. But they ought to have consulted him. (Haydock)

VERSE 35

Rose up; being oppressed with grief and wine, which would not excuse him from sin, particularly this second time. (Menochius)

VERSE 37

Elder. She first proposes: she is not ashamed to call her child *Moab,* "from father." The younger is rather more modest, and calls her son Ammon, "my people," not born of the Sodomites. Many reasons might be alleged to extenuate, or even to excuse the conduct of Lot and his daughters, as many of the fathers have done. But the Scripture barely leaves it upon record, without either commendation or blame. (Haydock)

CHAPTER XX

VERSE 1

Gerara; at a greater distance from the devoted country of Sodom. (Haydock)

VERSE 2

He said to the king, and to all others who made inquiry, as it was his custom, whenever he came into a strange land, ver. 13. He was encouraged to do this, by the protection which God had shown him in Egypt. --- *Took her,* against her will, as Pharao had done. (Haydock) --- Though she was ninety years old, and with child, her beauty was still extraordinary, the Rabbin think miraculous. At that time people lived above 120 years; so that at the age of ninety, she would only be about as near the end of her life as our women are at forty; and we often see people sufficiently attracting at that age. (Calmet)

VERSE 3

Abimelech. This was an usual title of kings in Chanaan, and a very good one, to remind them and their subjects, of their obligations, (Haydock) as it means "my father the king." The behavior of the prince shows, that as yet all sense of duty and knowledge of the true God was not banished from the country. (Calmet) --- *Shalt die,* unless thou restore the woman, whom thou hast taken by force; on whose account I have already afflicted thee, (ver. 7, 17.) and thus prevented thee from touching her. This testimony was more requisite, that there might be no doubt respecting Isaac's legitimacy. (Haydock)

VERSE 5

He say, &c. The pronouns in Hebrew are printed very incorrectly. --- *He is my sister; and she, even he, said.* (Kennicott)

VERSE 6

Sincere heart, abhorring adultery, but not altogether innocent. (Menochius)

VERSE 7

A prophet. One under my particular care, to whom I reveal many things. --- *He shall pray for thee.* Behold, God will sometimes grant, at the request of his saints, what he would deny even such as Abimelech or the friends of Job. Is not this sufficient encouragement for us, to have recourse to the intercession of the saints? And can anyone be so foolish as to pretend this is making gods of them, and showing them an idolatrous worship? (Haydock)

VERSE 8

In the night, (de nocte) or "as soon as it began to dawn." (Septuagint)

VERSE 9

Why, &c. He expostulates with him in a friendly but earnest manner. --- *A great sin,* or punishment, (Menochius) ver. 18, and exposed me to the danger of committing adultery. Abraham might have answered, this would have been his own fault, as he could not have done it without offering violence to Sara, in whose chastity he could confide. Having an opportunity here to vindicate himself, Abraham speaks freely, which he was not allowed to do in Egypt, chap. xii. 20.

VERSE 12

My sister, or niece, according to those who say she was daughter of Aran, who thus must have had a different mother from Abraham; (Menochius) or, as we rather think, Sara was *truly* his *half-sister,* born of Thare by another wife. His adding *truly,* seems to restrain it to this sense; and we know that in those countries, marriages of such near relations were allowed, though not when both had the same parents. Why should we not, therefore, believe Abraham, who certainly knew the real state of the question, and who would not tell a lie, rather than seek for improbable and far-fetched solutions? Said, who lived eight hundred years ago, mentions the name of Jona, Abraham's mother, as well as that of Tehevita, who bore Sara to Thare. The Hebrews, in general, give this explanation. (Calmet) --- By calling Sara his sister without any addition, Abraham intended that the people should conclude he was not married; therefore he did not say she was his half-sister, as this would have frustrated his design, if, as Clement of Alexandria, asserts, such might and did marry under the law of nature. (Haydock) --- Philo observes, the Athenian legislator, Solon, sanctioned the same practice, which was followed also by the Phœnicians. (Calmet)

VERSE 14

Gave, by way of satisfaction, for having detained his wife; as also to show his respect for him who was a prophet. (1 Kings ix. 7.) (Haydock)

VERSE 16

Thy brother, as thou hast agreed to call thy husband. --- *Pieces,* or sicles *of silver,* worth a little above 2s. 3d. each; total £113 sterling. --- *A covering,* or veil, to show thou art married, and prevent thee from being *taken* by any one hereafter. It was to be so rich, that all might know her quality. St. Paul (1 Corinthians xi. 5, 15.) orders women to be *covered.* (Calmet)

VERSE 17

Healed. It is not known how God afflicted Abimelech; but the women could not be delivered during the short time that Sara was detained: on her being set at liberty, *they bore children.* (Menochius)

CHAPTER XXI

VERSE 1

Visited, either by the angel, chap. xviii. 10, or by enabling her to have what he had promised, at the return of the season.

VERSE 3

Isaac. This word signifies *laughter;* (Challoner) or "he shall laugh," and be the occasion of joy to many, as St. John the Baptist was, Luke i. 14; and thus Sara seems to explain it, ver. 6.

VERSE 7

Gave suck; a certain proof that the child was born of her. (Menochius) ---*His old age,* when both the parents were far advanced in years, ver. 2. The mother being ninety at this time, would render the event most surprising. (Haydock)

VERSE 8

Weaned. St. Jerome says when he was five years old, though some said twelve. The age of men being prolonged, their infancy continued longer. One of the Machabees suckled her child three years, 2 Machabees vii. 27. (2 Paralipomenon xxxi. 16.) (Calmet) --- *Feast.* The life of the child being now considered in less danger. From the time of conception till this place, the husband kept at a distance from his wife. (Clement of Alexandria, strom. iii.) Samuel's mother made a feast or present when she weaned him, 1 Kings i. 24. (Menochius)

VERSE 9

Playing, or persecuting, as St. Paul explains it, Galatians iv. 29. The play tended to pervert the morals of the young Isaac, whether we understand this term *metsachak,* as implying idolatry, or obscene actions, or fighting; in all which senses it is used in Scripture. See Exodus xxxii. 6; Genesis xxvi. 8; 2 Kings ii. 14.) (Menochius) --- Ismael was 13 years older than Isaac; and took occasion, perhaps, from the *feast,* and other signs of preference given by his parents to the latter, to hate and persecute him, which Sara soon perceiving, was forced to have recourse to the expedient apparently so harsh, of driving Ismael and his mother from the house, that they might have an establishment of their own, and not disturb Isaac in the inheritance after the death of Abraham. (Haydock) --- In this she was guided by a divine light; (Menochius) and not by any female antipathy, ver. 12. Many of the actions of worldlings, which at first sight may appear innocent, have a natural and fatal tendency to pervert the morals of the just; and therefore, we must keep as much as possible at a distance from their society. --- *With Isaac her son.* Hebrew has simply *mocking,* without mentioning what. But the sequel shows the true meaning; and this addition was found in some Bibles in the days of St. Jerome, as he testifies, and is expressed in the Septuagint. (Haydock) --- Ismael was a figure of the synagogue, which persecuted the Church of Christ in her birth. (Du Hamel)

VERSE 11

For his son. He does not express any concern for Agar. But we cannot doubt but he would feel to part with her also. It was prudent to let both go together and the mother had perhaps encouraged Ismael, at least by neglecting to punish or watch over him, and so deserved to share in his affliction.

VERSE 14

Bread and water. This seems a very slender allowance to be given by a man of Abraham's riches. But he might intend her to go only into the neighborhood, where he would take care to provide for her. She lost herself in the wilderness, and thus fell into imminent danger of perishing. (Haydock) --- This divorce of Agar, and ejection of Ismael, prefigured the reprobation of the Jews.

VERSE 17

Of the boy, who was 17 years old, and wept at the approach of death. --- *Fear not.* Ye are under the protection of God, who will not abandon you, when all human succor fails; nor will he neglect his promises. (chap. 16.) (Haydock)

VERSE 20

Wilderness, in Arabia Petrea. --- *An archer,* living on plunder. (Calmet)

VERSE 22

Abimelech, king of Gerara, who knew that Abraham was a prophet, and a favorite of God, chap. xx. 7. (Haydock)

VERSE 23

Hurt me. Hebrew, "lie unto me," or revolt and disturb the peace of my people.

VERSE 24

I will swear. The matter was of sufficient importance. Abraham binds himself, but not his posterity, who by God's order fought against the descendants of this king.

VERSE 27

Gave them; thus rendering good for evil. (Du Hamel)

VERSE 31

Bersabee. That is, *the well of oath;* (Challoner) or "the well of the seven;" meaning the seven ewe-lambs set apart. (Menochius) --- This precaution of Abraham, in giving seven lambs as a testimony that the well was dug by him, was not without reason.

VERSE 33

A grove: in the midst of which was an altar, dedicated to the *Lord God eternal;* to testify that he alone was incapable of change. Thither Abraham frequently repaired, to thank God for all his favors. Temples were not probably as yet known in any part of the world. The ancient saints, Abraham, Isaac, Josue, &c., were pleased to show their respect for God, and their love of retirement, by planting groves, and consecrating altars to the supreme Deity. If this laudable custom was afterwards perverted by the idolaters, and hence forbidden to God's people, we need not wonder. The best things may be abused; and when they become a source of scandal, we must avoid them. (Haydock) --- (Josue xxix. 26; Deuteronomy xvi. 23; Judges vi. 25.)

CHAPTER XXII
VERSE 1

God tempted, &c. God *tempteth no man to evil,* James i. 13. But by trial and experiment, maketh known to the world and to ourselves, what we are; as here by this trial the singular faith and obedience of Abraham was made manifest. (Challoner)

VERSE 2

Thy only begotten, or thy most beloved, as if he had been an only child; in which sense the word is often taken, 1 Paralipomenon xxix. 1. Ismael was still living; but Isaac was the only son of Sara, the most dignified wife. ---*Lovest.* Hebrew, "hast loved" hitherto; now thou must consider him as dead. He has been to thee a source of joy, but now he will be one of tears and mourning. --- *Of vision.* Septuagint, "high" being situated on Mount Moria, by which name it was afterwards distinguished, ver. 14. (Menochius) --- Every word in this astonishing command, tended to cut Abraham to the heart; and thence we may the more admire his strength and disinterestedness of his faith. He could hope, in a manner, against hope, knowing in whom he had trusted, and convinced that God would not deceive him, though he was at a loss to explain in what manner Isaac should have children after he was sacrificed. (Haydock)

VERSE 3

In the night: de nocte, Hebrew, "very early in the morning." --- *His son,* 25 years old, without perhaps saying a word to Sara about the intended sacrifice; though some believe, he had too great an opinion of her faith and constancy, not to reveal to her the order of God. The Scripture is silent. (Calmet)

VERSE 5

Will return. He hoped, perhaps, that God would restore Isaac to life: (Hebrews xi. 19) and he could not well express himself otherwise to the men, who were not acquainted with the divine decree. (Calmet)

VERSE 7

Holocaust. These were probably the only sacrifices yet in use. (Calmet) --- The conversation of Isaac could not fail to pierce the heart of his father. (Menochius)

VERSE 9

The place. Mount Moria, on part of which the temple was built afterwards; and on another part, called Calvary, our Savior was crucified, having carried his cross, as Isaac did the wood for sacrifice. --- *His son:* having first explained to him the will of God, to which Isaac gave his free consent; otherwise, being in the vigor of his youth, he might easily have hindered his aged father, who was 125 years old, from binding him. But in this willingness to die, as in many other particulars, he was a noble figure of Jesus Christ, who was *offered because it was His will.* (Haydock)

VERSE 10

To sacrifice; a thing hitherto unprecedented, and which God would never suffer to be done in his honor, though he was pleased to try the obedience of his servant so far. The pagans afterwards took occasion, perhaps, from this history, to suppose, that human victims would be the most agreeable to their false deities: (Calmet) but in this misconception they were inexcusable, since God prevented the sacrifice from being really offered to him, in the most earnest manner, *saying, Abraham, Abraham,* as if there were danger lest the holy man should not hear the first call. (Haydock)

VERSE 12

Hast not spared. Thus the intentions of the heart become worthy of praise, or of blame, even when no exterior effect is perceived. (Haydock)

VERSE 13

He took; God having given him the dominion over it. (Calmet)

VERSE 14

Will see. This became a proverbial expression, used by people in distress, who, remembering how Abraham had been relieved, endeavored to comfort themselves with hopes of relief. Some translate *the Lord will be seen,* which was verified when Christ was crucified. (Menochius) --- Or, he *will provide,* alluding to what was said, ver. 8.

VERSE 16

Own self; as he could not swear by any one greater. (Hebrews vi. 13; Jeremias xxii. 5.)

Stars and dust, comprising the just and sinners. --- *Gates,* shall judge and rule. (Haydock)

VERSE 20

Children. These are mentioned here, to explain the marriage of Isaac with Rebecca, the grand-daughter of Nachor and Melcha.

VERSE 21

Hus, who peopled Ausitis in Arabia, the desert, where Job lived. --- *Buz,* from whom sprung *Elihu the Busite,* the Balaam of the Jews. (St. Jerome) --- *Syrians,* called Camiletes, to the west of the Euphrates; or father of the Cappadocians. (Calmet)

VERSE 24

Concubine, or wife, secondary in privileges, love, and dignity. Though Nachor did not, perhaps imitate the faith and virtue of his brother Abraham, but mixed various superstitions with the knowledge of the true God; yet we need not condemn him, for having more wives than one. (Haydock)

CHAPTER XXIII
VERSE 1

Sara. She is the only woman whose age the Scripture specifies; a distinction which her exalted dignity and faith deserved. (Galatians iv. 23; Hebrews xi. 11.) She was a figure of the Christian Church. (Calmet)

VERSE 2

City. Hebrew, Cariath *arbah,* Josue xiv. 15. --- *Which is Hebron.* Serarius thinks it took its name from the *society* (cherber) between Abraham and the princes of the city. Hebron the son of Caleb possessed it afterwards. ---*Came* from Bersabee, (chap. xxii. 19.) or to the place where the corpse lay, at Arbee, which signifies *four;* as Adam, Abraham, Isaac, and Jacob, with their four wives, reposed there. (Calmet) --- *And weep.* In the middle of this word, in the printed Hebrew, there is left a small c; whence the Rabbins ridiculously infer, that Abraham wept but a short time. But the retaining of *greater, less, suspended and inverted* letters in the Hebrew Bible, can be attributed to no other cause than a scrupulous veneration even for the faults of transcribers. (Kennicott)

VERSE 3

Obsequies, or solemn mourning, accompanied with prayer. (Acts viii. 2; Matthew xii.) The Jews are still accustomed to say, when they bury their dead, "Ye fathers, who sleep in Hebron, open to him the gates of Eden;" herein agreeing with the Catholic doctrine, as they did in the days of Judas the Machabee. (Haydock)

VERSE 6

Prince of God, powerful and holy, and worthy of respect. (Haydock) --- A great prince. See Acts vii. 5, where St. Stephen says, that God did not give Abraham a foot of land, meaning as an inheritance; and that Abraham bought this double cave, for a sepulcher, of the sons of *Hemor,* the son of *Sichem;* (Calmet) from which latter he seems to derive the name of the place, which is here called Hebron. (Haydock) --- Nothing is more common, than for men and places to have two names; though some think, the name of Abraham has been inserted in the Acts by a mistake of the copyists, when Jacob was meant. See chap. xxxiii. 19. (Calmet)

VERSE 7

Bowed down to the people. Adoravit, literally, *adored.* But this word here, as well as in many other places in the Latin Scriptures, is used to signify only an inferior honor and reverence paid to men, expressed by a bowing down of the body.

VERSE 16

Sicles. About £50. (Haydock) --- It was no simony to buy land for a sepulcher, as it was not blessed. (Menochius) --- *Current money,* was such as passed among merchants, though probably not yet coined in any part of the world; and therefore we find, that Abraham and others weigh the pieces of silver or gold. In this manner were bargains concluded before witnesses, who in those days supplied the want of writings and lawyers. (Calmet)

CHAPTER XXIV
VERSE 2

Servant. Eliezer, or Damascus, whom he had once intended for his heir, chap. xv. 2. (Haydock) --- *Under, &c.* either to show their subjection, (Sa.) or their faith in Christ, who should be born of Abraham, (St. Jerome, ep. 140) or to testify that their oath shall be no less binding than the covenant of circumcision. For this last reason, the Jews still observe the custom of sitting upon the hand of the person who takes an oath. (Menochius) See chap. xlvii. 29, where Jacob imitates the action of his grand-father. These two patriarchs, progenitors of Christ are the only ones in Scripture whom we find practicing it; whence St. Augustine and St. Ambrose conclude, that it had a reference to the mysterious birth or our Redeemer. (Bonfrere.)

VERSE 4

Country. Huran, where Abraham had dwelt with Thare, &c. There Nachor's family still resided, and had more respect for the true God than the Chanaanites, (Haydock) though they gave way to some sort of idolatry. (Menochius) --- Hence Abraham was in hopes that a partner worthy of Isaac might be found among his relations, better than among those devoted nations; and thus he has left an instruction to all parents, to be solicitous for the real welfare of their children; and to dissuade them earnestly from marrying with infidels; a thing which God forbade in the old law, as the Church still does in the new. (Haydock)

VERSE 5

If the woman. Thus he shows his religious respect for an oath; and will not depend on his own explanation of the sense of it. (Calmet)

VERSE 7

He will send his angel before thee. This shows that the Hebrews believed that God gave them guardian angels for their protection. (Challoner) ---*Angel.* A proof of the antiquity of our belief respecting angel guardians. (Calmet)

VERSE 14

By this. He chose a mark which would manifest the kindness and humility of the maid, who would be a fit match for the pious Isaac. This was no vain observation. God heard his fervent prayer. (St. Chrysostom) (Calmet) --- It is sometimes lawful to ask a sign or miracle of God, (Acts i. 24; iv. 30; 1 Kings xiv, &c.,) but we must carefully avoid whatever the Church disapproves. (St. Augustine de Gen. ii. 17; xii. 22.) (Worthington)

VERSE 21

To know, though he was now almost convinced, that this obliging virgin was the person of whom he was in quest; and hence he proceeds to make her presents of great value. (Haydock)

VERSE 27

Mercy and truth: or a real kindness, so often mentioned in the Psalms. (Calmet)

VERSE 41

Curse, which always attends the person who does not endeavor to comply with a lawful oath. (Haydock) --- The Hebrews commonly added in this sense, *May God do these things to me, and still more,* if I prove false. (Menochius) --- In this sense, Abraham's steward gives the meaning of his master, as he had hitherto repeated his very words at full length. This perfectly agrees with the style of the heroic ages; such as we find expressed in the poems of Homer, the most ancient work of any heathen author. The account which he gives of the noble simplicity of those ages, when the ladies went for water, and princes prepared the entertainments for their guests, cannot fail to strike us, when we compare the works of that admired author with the inspired writings. (Haydock)

VERSE 49

Left, in quest of some other lady of my master's kindred; as some of Bathuel's brothers might also have children. He was the youngest. (Haydock)

VERSE 50

Laban is placed before his father, having perhaps the administration of affairs in Bathuel's old age; and he had first introduced the stranger. (Menochius)

VERSE 53

Present. Thus ratifying what he had already done, (ver. 22,) and obtaining full consent, both of the virgin, and of her father and brother.

VERSE 54

Morning. He loses no time to afford comfort to his masters, and to give proof that he was not esteemed by them without reason.

VERSE 57

Let us call the maid, and ask her will. Not as to her marriage, as she had already consented, but of her quitting her parents and going to her husband. (Challoner)

VERSE 58

I will go, without delay, being well convinced that the good steward was directed by God. Hence she was guilty of no imprudence or levity, in yielding herself up to the divine will, and consenting so readily to the proposed marriage.

VERSE 62

The well of Agar, not far from Bersabee.

VERSE 63

To meditate on the obligations of the state on which he was about to enter, and on other pious subjects, free from noise and distraction. (Haydock) --- In profane authors, the word used by the Septuagint means to talk about trifles, &c. (Calmet) --- But the known piety of Isaac, and the authority of that version, forbid that we should take it here in that sense. (Haydock)

VERSE 65

Cloak, or summer veil, covering the whole body, and having an opening only for the eyes; such as the Eastern ladies use. St. Jerome in Isai. iii, Rebecca does this out of modesty. (Haydock) --- She prefigures the Gentiles, whom Jesus calls by his servants laden with his gifts, to become his spouse, or his Church, (Calmet) at the *fountain* of baptism. He adorns her with the *ear-rings* of obedience, and the *bracelets* of good works. (Du Hamel)

VERSE 67

Mother's death, which happened about three years before. (Menochius) --- Isaac was now forty years old, and yet he does not pretend to take a wife for himself; leaving the choice to his good father, and to God. (Du Hamel)

CHAPTER XXV
VERSE 1

Cetura, his third wife; the former two being perhaps both dead. This Abraham did in his 137th year, that God might have witnesses also among the Gentiles. Cetura was before one of his handmaids. (Menochius) --- God enabled him to have children at this advanced age; or perhaps, Moses may have related his marriage in this place, though it had taken place several years before. (St. Augustine, contra Jul. iii.) (Calmet) This learned father, City of God xvi. 34, supposes that the reason why Cetura is styled a concubine, though she was a lawful and only wife, is because her children prefigured heretics, who do not belong to the kingdom of Christ. (Worthington)

VERSE 6

Concubines. Agar and Cetura are here called *concubines,* (though they were lawful wives, and in other places are so called) because they were of an inferior degree and such in Scripture are usually called concubines. (Challoner) --- The solemnities of marriage were omitted on these occasions, and the children were not entitled to a share in the inheritance. Jacob's two wives consented that all his children, by their handmaids, should be placed on the same footing with their own. (Calmet) --- Abraham contented himself with making suitable *presents* to the children, whom he had by these secondary wives, reserving the bulk of his property to Isaac, chap. xxiv. 36. He also provided for their establishment himself, that there might be no contest after his departure.

VERSE 8

Good old age. Because well spent: though he lived not so long as many of the wicked; *decaying* not by any violent disorder, but dropping off like a ripe apple. --- *Being full.* The Hebrew does not express of what; but the Samaritan, Chaldean, Septuagint, Syriac, and

Arabic agree with the Vulgate. See chap. xxxv. 29. (Haydock) --- *Days,* not *years,* as Protestants wrongfully interpolate. (Kennicott) --- *His people,* the saints of ancient days, in limbo; while his body was placed near the remains of his wife, by the pious attention of his two chief sons, attended by their other brethren. (Haydock) --- The life of Abraham was a pattern of all virtues, but particularly of faith; and it was an abridgment of the law. His equal was no where found, Ecclesiasticus xliv. 20. (Calmet)

VERSE 16

By their castles; or, the castles, towns, and tribes of principal note, received their names from these twelve princes, or phylarks, whose authority is still recognized among all the tribes of the Arabs. (Thevenot.) (Haydock) --- The towns of these people were easily built, and more easily destroyed; for they consisted only of tents, Jeremias xlix. 31. Their castles were perhaps only *sheep-folds,* as the original *Tiroth* may signify; or they were a sort of watch-towers, to prevent the sudden attack of an invading enemy, and to serve also for a retreat. (Calmet)

VERSE 18

In the presence, &c. As he was the eldest, so he died first; having lived unmolested and fearless among his father's children, chap. xvi. 12. (Calmet)

VERSE 21

Barren. They had been married 20 years, (ver. 26.) during which time, St. Chrysostom says, Isaac had earnestly besought the Lord, (Menochius) and obtained by prayer what God long before decreed. See St. Gregory, Dial. i. 8. (Worthington)

VERSE 22

To be so. That is, if I must die, and my children also. She feared the worst; and immediately had recourse to the Lord, either in her oratory, or at one of his altars erected by Abraham; and received a gracious answer from him by means of an angel. (Haydock) --- Others think she consulted Melchisedech at Mount Moria. (Menochius)

VERSE 23

The younger. The Idumeans shall be subdued by the arms of David: and the Jews themselves shall yield to the Christian Church. (St. Augustine, City of God xvi. 35.) St. Paul, Romans ix, draws another very important truth from this history, showing the mercy of God to be gratuitous in choosing his saints. (Worthington)

VERSE 25

Red. Hence he was called Edom, as well as from the red pottage, ver. 30. (Haydock) ---
Hairy like a skin. On which account Rebecca afterwards clothed Jacob's hands and neck with the
skins of kids, to make him resemble Esau. Furry robes were not unusual among the Jews. Some
imagine that the name of *Sehar,* was given to Esau, on account of his being *hairy* but *Esau* was
the title by which he was commonly known, and it means *one made perfect;* because he came
into the world, "covered with hair like a man." --- *Jacob:* "a supplanter, or wrestler." (Calmet) ---
From the birth of these twins St. Gregory shows the folly of astrologers, who pretend that our
actions are under the influence of the planets; and that two, born at the same moment, will have
the same fate. How different were the lives of Jacob and Esau! (Haydock)

VERSE 27

A husbandman: a rustic, both in profession and manners, like Cain; while Jacob was a
shepherd, in imitation of Abel, plain and honest. (Haydock)

VERSE 28

Loved Esau, as his first-born, who showed him all attention, and whom he would
naturally have appointed his heir, if the will of God had not afterwards been revealed to him.
Rebecca, to whom this was already known, gave the preference in her love to Jacob. (Haydock)

VERSE 29

Pottage, of Egyptian lentiles, the most excellent in the world. (Calmet)

VERSE 30

Give me, &c. Hebrew, "make me devour this red;" which denotes, the very red quality of
the pottage, and the greediness of Esau. (Calmet)

VERSE 31

Sell me. He had been informed by his mother, that God had transferred the *birth-right* to
him; and, therefore, he takes this opportunity to obtain the consent of Esau quietly. The latter,
who knew nothing of God's decree, showed his little regard for that privilege. (Haydock) --- He
perhaps intended to assert his claim by force, notwithstanding this agreement. (Menochius) --- It
is not probable that he could plead in earnest, that he was famishing in the midst of his father's
house. (Du Hamel) --- The birth-right was a temporal honor; though some assert that the office
of priesthood belonged also to it. This, however, does not seem to be certain; for we find Abel,
Abraham, and other younger children offering sacrifice. The first-born were entitled to a double
portion, (Deuteronomy xxi. 17; 1 Paralipomenon v. 2, 5) and to their father's peculiar blessing,

Ecclesiasticus iii. 12. To despise such advantages betrayed a bad disposition, for which Esau is condemned, Hebrews xii. 16; Romans ix. (Calmet) --- Jacob's conduct was perfectly innocent, whether we consider this transaction as serious or not. Isaac never ratified the bargain; nor do we find that Jacob rested his claim on it. (Haydock) --- But it is recorded by Moses, to show the disposition of these two young men. (Calmet)

VERSE 33

Swore; and still we find him enraged above measure, when Isaac had, by mistake, ratified the transfer of the birth-right to Jacob; (chap. xxvii. 41.) whence we may gather, that he did not intend to perform what he promised, even with the solemnity of an oath; which renders him still more deserving of the title *profane,* which St. Paul gives him. (Haydock)

CHAPTER XXVI

VERSE 5

Ceremonies of religion, observed under the law of nature. (Menochius)

VERSE 7

Sister, or niece. Though lawful at that time, it was not very common for people to marry such near relations; and therefore Isaac, by saying Rebecca was his sister, wished the people of Gerara to be ignorant of her being his wife; being under the like apprehension as his father had been twice before. He imitates his example, trusting in the protection of God, which had rescued Abraham from danger, chap. xxi. (Haydock)

VERSE 8

His wife; using greater familiarity that a grave and virtuous man, like Isaac, would offer to do with his sister, or with another person's wife. --- *Sin,* or punishment, (Menochius) such as Abimelech's father had formerly experienced. (Haydock)

VERSE 11

Touch, or hurt, by offering to marry, &c. (Haydock) --- Adultery was punished with death among these nations, chap. xxxviii. 24, as it was by the law of Moses. (Calmet)

VERSE 12

And the Lord. This is not mentioned as a miracle; for Egypt and many other countries produced 100 fold. Pliny, Natural History xviii. 10, says, some parts of Africa rendered 150 times as much as was sowed. The famine had now ceased. (Calmet)

VERSE 16

Depart. Instead of repressing the outrages of his subjects, the king enters into their jealousies, and banishes a wealthy person, (Haydock) as the Athenians so frequently did afterwards with respect to their best citizens. (Aristotle, Polit. iii. 9.) --- And Pharao used the same pretext, when he persecuted the Hebrews. (Calmet)

VERSE 18

Servants. So the Septuagint and Syriac versions, and the Samaritan copy against the Hebrew, *in the days,* which is incorrect. (Kennicott)

VERSE 19

Torrent. That is, a channel where sometimes a torrent, or violent stream had run. (Challoner) --- In this vale of Gerara, a never-failing spring was found. (Haydock)

VERSE 22

Latitude. That is, wideness, or room. (Challoner) --- Hebrew *Reheboth,* widely extended streams, *latitudes.*

VERSE 24

Of Abraham, who still lives before me, and for whom I always testified such affection, though I suffered him to be persecuted: hence, *fear not.* (Haydock)

VERSE 26

Ochozath. This name occurs in the Septuagint, as well as the other two; (chap. xxi. 22.) and means *a company of friends.* Phicol also signifies *the mouth* or *face of all,* being the general of the army on whom the soldiers must be intent. These are, perhaps, therefore, the names of offices, not of persons; or if they be the same who lived with Abraham, they must have held their high command above 100 years. (Menochius) (Calmet)

VERSE 35

Offended. They were the daughters of princes of the Heathens, (Josephus) and being brought up in idolatry and pride, refused to give ear to the advice of Isaac, who never approved of the marriage of his son with them. Esau would not leave the choice of a wife to his father, as Isaac had done at the same age. (Haydock)

CHAPTER XXVII
VERSE 1

Old: 137 years, when falling sickly and blind, at least for a time, he wished to bless Esau, who was 77 years old. (Tirinus)

VERSE 4

That, &c. He does not mean, that the meat would induce him to give his blessing. Neither can we suppose, that he intended to pervert the order of God, in making the younger son subject to the elder, if he was informed by Rebecca, of that disposition of providence. (Calmet) --- But of this he seems to have been ignorant, ver. 29, 35. (Worthington)

VERSE 7

In the sight of the Lord, answers to *my soul,* &c., ver. 4. I will bless thee with all earnestness and sincerity. (Haydock)

VERSE 12

Mocked him, taking advantage of his blindness and old age. (Menochius)

VERSE 13

This curse. Rebecca had too much confidence in God's promises, to think that he would suffer them to be ineffectual. Hence, Onkelos makes her say, "I have learnt by revelation, that thou wilt receive no curse, but only blessing." The sequel showed, that she was directed by God in this delicate business. (Theodoret, q. 78.) (Calmet)

VERSE 15

Very good. Hebrew *desirable,* kept among perfumes, ver. 27. Such, the Hebrews say, were used by the first-born, when they offered sacrifice. (St. Jerome, q. Hebrews.)

VERSE 19

I am Esau, thy first-born. St. Augustine, (L. *Contra Mendacium,* c. x..) treating at large upon this place, excuse Jacob from a lie, because this whole passage was mysterious, as relating to the preference which was afterwards to be given to the Gentiles before the carnal Jews, which Jacob by prophetic light might understand. So far is certain, that the first birth-right, both by divine election, and by Esau's free cession, belonged to Jacob: so that if there were any lie in the case, it could be no more than an officious and venial one. (Challoner) --- Ignorance might also excuse them from any sin; as many good and learned men have thought an officious lie to be lawful. (St. Chrysostom, hom. 52; Origen; Bonfrere.) And even if we allow that they did wrong; the Scripture relates, but does not sanction what they did, *Let him that thinks himself to stand, take heed lest he fall,* 1 Corinthians x. 12. (Calmet) --- As our Savior says of St. John the Baptist, *He is Elias,* Matthew xi, so, Jacob says, *I am Esau,* not in person but in right of the first-born. (Worthington)

VERSE 22

Of Esau. Thus, too often our voice contradicts our hands or actions! (Haydock)

VERSE 27

Plentiful. A word retained by the Samaritan and Septuagint though lost in the Hebrew copies. (Grotius.) ---*Hath blessed* with abundance of fruit and odoriferous herbs; such as had probably been shut up in the drawers with Esau's robes. (Menochius)

VERSE 28

Wine. "By which Christ gathers together the multitude, in the Sacrament of his Body and Blood." (St. Augustine)

VERSE 29

Worship thee, with civil respect, (Haydock) as the Idumeans, Philistines and Moabites did, with respect to David, Solomon, and the Macabees, acknowledging their dominion, though reluctantly. --- *With blessing.* Thus Rebecca had not given her son a vain assurance. Isaac prays that God may ever by his protector, and avenge his cause. (Haydock)

VERSE 33

Fear. Septuagint, "Isaac was rapt into an ecstasy exceedingly great;" during which God explained to him the meaning of what had happened, that he might not think of revoking his blessing. (St. Augustine, q. 80.) He permitted Isaac to be in darkness respecting this affair, that it might be more manifest, that the will of man had no part in preferring Jacob; (St. Chrysostom, hom. 53) and that Esau might not direct his rage against his father. (Worthington) --- *Be blessed.* Thus he confirms what he had done; and shows that he bore no resentment towards his younger son, nor esteemed himself to be mocked, ver. 12. (Haydock)

VERSE 34

Roared, through savage fury and envy of his brother. (Eusebius) (Menochius)

VERSE 35

Deceitfully. Hebrew, slyly; directed by *wisdom,* as the Chaldean has it. St. Chrysostom (de sacred) praises the address of Jacob on this occasion. (Calmet)

VERSE 36

Jacob. That is, a *supplanter.* (Challoner) --- *My blessing.* Both Isaac and Esau speak of this blessing, according to the dictates of nature. But God had disposed of it otherwise. The profane and cruel manners of Esau rendered him unworthy of it; and he could not maintain his natural claim, after having freely resigned it even with an oath. He seems to distinguish the blessing from the birth-right, though one necessarily followed the other. (Haydock)

VERSE 37

Brethren, or relations; (Menochius) for Isaac had no other children but these two. He never married any other woman but the beautiful and virtuous Rebecca. (Haydock)

VERSE 39

Moved; yet not so as to repent of what he had done; for Esau *found no place of repentance* in his father's breast, *although with tears he had sought it,* (Hebrew xii. 17) desiring to obtain the blessing of the first-born. (Haydock) --- *In the fat,* &c. Idumea was a barren country; and hence some would translate the Hebrew, "far from the fat...shall they dwelling be; but thou shalt live by the sword." Thus *min* often means *from,* as well as for *in: my flesh is changed on account of* the want of *oil,* Psalm cviii. 24. Hebrew, *a pinguedine.* (Calmet) --- But all the ancient versions agree with the Vulgate. So that we may say, the blessing of God made those barren regions supply the wants of the people abundantly; and so the Idumeans were to live by the sword, they would seize the rich habitations of their neighbors, (Haydock) and thus obtain a country rendered fertile without their labor. (Menochius)

VERSE 40

Thy brother, in the reign of David, 2 Kings viii. 14 and of the Machabees. (Josephus, Antiquities xiii. 17.) --- *Yoke.* When the house of Juda shall rebel against the Lord, in the days of

Joram, then the Idumeans shall regain their liberty for a time; (4 Kings viii. 20) to be subdued again after 800 years by John Hyrcan, the high priest. (Haydock) --- All the blessing of Esau tends to confirm that already given to his brother; so that the apostle seems to have considered it unworthy of notice. (Calmet) --- Jacob, in the mean time, never asserted his dominion; but still called Esau his lord, (chap. xxxii. 4) and behaved to him with the greatest deference. (Haydock) --- Yet the Idumeans always hated the Jews, and assisted Titus to destroy Jerusalem. (Josephus) (Tirinus)

VERSE 41

My father. He has no regard for this mother. (Menochius) --- Her love for Jacob filled him with greater indignation; and he resolved to murder him, in order, perhaps, to revenge himself on both. Though this cruel resolution was taken *in his heart,* with full deliberation, he was not so careful to conceal his intentions; but his watchful mother discovered it, and by her prudence, preserved him from committing the external sin: and Jacob from falling a prey to this second Cain.

VERSE 45

Both my sons. Esau would have forfeited his life for murder, chap. ix. 6. (Haydock) --- Perhaps she might also fear that Jacob, in his own defense, should in the very agony of death, give the aggressor a mortal wound; or that Esau, at least, would be forced to flee his country. Indeed, she considered him already as a lost man, on account of his marriage with the two women of Chanaan, and his savage manners. (Calmet)

VERSE 46

To live. Life will be a burden to me. (Menochius) --- She does not mention the principal reason of her desiring Jacob to go to Haran, for fear of grieving the tender heart of her husband; who, it seems, knew not the temper of Esau so well as she did. (Calmet)

CHAPTER XXVIII

VERSE 2

Take. Septuagint, "flee;" as if Isaac began at last to be apprized of Esau's designs. Wisdom (x. 10) *conducted the just when he fled from his brother's wrath,* &c. --- *Thy uncle.* He points out the house, but leaves the woman to his choice.

VERSE 4

Grandfather. Isaac, out of modesty, does not mention that the same promises had been made to himself. He determines the right over Chanaan to belong solely to Jacob, and to his posterity. (Haydock)

VERSE 9

To Ismael's family; for he had been dead fourteen years. Esau asks no advice. It is doubtful whether he meant to appease or irritate his parents, (Menochius) by this marriage with the daughter of Ismael. She lived with her brother, the head of the Nabutheans, and is called Basemath, chap. xxxvi. 3. (Calmet)

VERSE 11

Head for a pillow. Behold the austerity of the heir of all that country! (Haydock) --- He departs from home in haste, with his staff only, that Esau might not know. (Worthington)

VERSE 12

A ladder and angels, &c. This mysterious vision tended to comfort the patriarch, with the assurance that God would now take him under his more particular protection, when he was destitute of human aid. (Haydock) --- The angels *ascending,* foretold that his journey would be prosperous; and *descending,* showed that he would return with safety. (Menochius) --- Or rather, the ladder represented the incarnation of Jesus Christ, born of so many patriarchs from Adam, who was created by God, to the blessed Virgin. He is the *way* by which we must ascend, by observing the *truth,* till we obtain *life* eternal. (Haydock) --- Mercy and truth are like the two sides; the virtues of Christ are signified by the steps. Angels descend to announces this joyful mystery to men; they ascend to convey the prayers and ardent desires of the ancient saints, to hasten their redemption. (Menochius) --- Our Savior seems to allude to this passage, John i. 51; xiv. 6. The Providence of God, watching over all things, appears here very conspicuous.

VERSE 13

Thy father, or grandfather. God joins the dead with the living, to show that all live to him, and that the soul is immortal. (Haydock)

VERSE 16

Knew it not. Jacob was not ignorant that God fills all places. But he thought that he would not manifest himself thus in a land given to idolatry. He begins to suspect that the place had been formerly consecrated to the worship of the true God, (Calmet) as it probably had by Abraham, who dwelt near Bethel, (chap. xii. 8) and built an altar on Mount Moria, chap. xxii. 14. Interpreters are not agreed on which of these places Jacob spent the night. St. Augustine, q. 83, supposes it was on the latter, "where God appointed the tabernacle to remain." The Chaldean paraphrases it very well in this sense, ver. 17, "How terrible is this place! It is not an ordinary place, but a place beloved by God and over against this place is the door of heaven." (Haydock)

VERSE 18

A title. That is a pillar or monument. (Challoner) --- Or an altar, consecrated by that rite to the service of the true God. This he did without any superstition; as the Catholic Church still pours oil or chrism upon her altars, in imitation of Jacob. (Raban. Instit. i. 45.) If pagans did the like, this is no reason why we should condemn the practice. They were blamable for designing thus to worship false gods. (Clement of Alexandria, strom. vii; Apul. Florid. i; &c.) If Protestants pull down altars, under the plea of their being superstitious, we cannot but pity their ignorance or malice. (Worthington)

VERSE 19

Bethel. This name signifies the house of God. (Challoner) --- Bethel was the name which Jacob gave to the place; and the town, which was built after his return, was called by the same name. Hence those famous animated stones or idols, received their title (*Bethules,* Eusebius, præp. i. 10.) being consecrated to Saturn, the Sun, &c. Till the days of Mahomet, the Arabs adored a rough stone, taken from the temple of Mecca, which they pretended was built by Abraham. (Chardin.) --- *Luza,* so called from the number of nut or almond trees. Here the golden calf was afterwards set up, on the confines of the tribes of Benjamin and of Ephraim, (Calmet) the southern limits of the kingdom of Jeroboam. (Haydock)

VERSE 20

A vow; not simply that he would acknowledge one God, but that he would testify his peculiar veneration for him, by erecting an altar, at his return, and by giving voluntarily the tithes of all he had. (Worthington) (chap. xxxv. 7.) How he gave these tithes, we do not read. Perhaps he might herby engage his posterity to give them under the law of Moses. (Calmet)

CHAPTER XXIX

VERSE 1

East. Mesopotamia, where Laban dwelt. (Haydock)

VERSE 2

Stone. Not of such an immoderate size but that Jacob could remove it. In that country water was scarce, and preserved with care. (Calmet)

VERSE 3

Sheep. Instead of this, Kennicott would read *shepherds;* as also ver. 2 and 8. In which last, the Samaritan, Arabic and Septuagint agree with him; as the two former do likewise in this third verse. (Haydock)

VERSE 4

Brethren. Jacob understands and speaks their language, either because it was not very different from his own, or he had learnt the Chaldean language from his mother. In the days of Ezechias, the Jews did not understand it. (4 Kings xviii. 26; Jeremias v. 15.) (Calmet)

VERSE 5

Of Nachor, by Bathuel, who was not so well known. (Menochius)

VERSE 6

Health. Hebrew, "in peace;" by which name all good things are designated. (Du Hamel)

VERSE 7

To feed. He shows his knowledge of pastoral affairs, and his concern for them. (Menochius)

VERSE 9

Hebrew He, ipsa. Eva is put for Eia, the letters being similar, chap. iii. 15. (Haydock) --- Other copies agree with the Vulgate and the Septuagint (Calmet)

VERSE 10

Cousin-german, and *uncle,* are put for brevity's sake by St. Jerome, instead of the Hebrew, "the daughter of Laban, brother of Rebecca his mother," and "his mother's brother." (Haydock)

VERSE 11

Kissed her, according to the custom of the country, (chap. xxiv. 26) having told her who he was. He was not so young, that she could suspect him guilty of an unbecoming levity, being above 77 years old, chap. xxvii. 1. (Haydock) --- In that age of simplicity, beautiful maids might converse with shepherds, without suspicion or danger. (Menochius) --- *Wept,* through tenderness, and perhaps on account of his present inability to make her a suitable present. (Calmet)

VERSE 12

Brother, or nephew. The name of brother, in Scripture, almost corresponds with the *Consanguineus* of the Latins, or our *relation.*

VERSE 14

My flesh, entitled to my utmost protection and friendship. (Calmet)

VERSE 17

Blear-eyed. Hebrew, racoth. Watery and tender, unable to look steadfastly at any object, but at the same time very *beautiful.* (Onkelos; &c.) --- The beauty of Rachel was perfect; not confined to one part. These two sisters represented the synagogue and the Church of Christ. Lia, though married first, never gains the entire affection of her husband. (Calmet)

VERSE 20

For Rachel. It was then the custom to buy or to pay a dowry for a wife. (chap. xxxiv. 12; Osee iii. 2.) Herodotus says, i. 196, that the Babylonians sold their beautiful women as high as possible, and gave part of the price to help off the more deformed. The Turks do the like. (Calmet) --- *A few,* &c. So highly did he esteem Rachel, that he thought he had obtained her for just nothing, though delays naturally seem long to lovers. (Tirinus) --- Calmet supposes that he was married to her the second month after he arrived at Haran; and on this account, easily explains his words, as love made all labor tolerable, and even easy, in the enjoyment of the beautiful Rachel. Usher also places the birth of Ruben in the first year of Jacob's service, A. 2246 [in the year of the world 2246]. But Salien and the context decide that he waited full seven years, and then obtained Lia, by fraud, of Laban; and seven days after, Rachel. (Haydock) --- He was then 84 years old! (Du Hamel)

VERSE 21

Go in, &c. To consummate my marriage; (Menochius) as the time is expired. (Haydock)

VERSE 22

Friends. Hebrew, Septuagint and Chaldean say, "all the men of that place." He was rich, and, though very greedy, could not well avoid conforming to the custom of making a splendid entertainment on such a joyful occasion. (Haydock)

VERSE 24

A handmaid, by way of dowry, as he did afterwards to Rachel. Both sisters considered it so small, as to say they had nothing, chap. xxxi. 14. --- *Lia,* who committed a great sin of adultery, though she was more excusable than Laban; inasmuch as she obeyed his order. (Menochius) --- Jacob might justly have refused to marry her; and then what a dishonor would have been entailed upon her for life! In consequence of this imposition, the legitimacy of Ruben's conception was rendered doubtful. We may suppose that shame hindered Lia from opening her mouth; so that Jacob had no means of discovering the cheat till day-break, having gone into the nuptial chamber after it was dark, according to custom, and the woman being also covered with a veil, Tobias viii. 1. Hence Jacob was guilty of no fault, as his mistake was involuntary. (Haydock) --- He afterwards consented to marry her, (Calmet) probably on the second day of the feast. (Haydock)

VERSE 26

Custom. This appears to be a false pretext: for all the people saw that Rachel was adorned like the intended bride, (Haydock) and were invited to her wedding. (Menochius)

VERSE 28

Week. Seven days; not years, as Josephus would have it. The nuptial feast lasted a week, Judges xiv. 15.

VERSE 30

Latter. Jacob is the figure of Jesus Christ; who rejected the synagogue, and treated his Church, gathered from all nations, with the utmost affection. (Calmet) --- Lia means "painful or laborious;" and Rachel a *sheep;* denoting, that a quiet contemplative life must be united with an active one; and that the Church must suffer here, and be crowned in heaven. (Haydock) (St. Gregory, Mor. vi. 28.)

VERSE 31

Despised, or loved less; so Christ orders us to *hate father,* &c., Matthew x. 17. (Calmet)

VERSE 32

Ruben. "See the son, *or* the son of vision;" alluding perhaps, distantly, to ver. 24, *He saw Lia.* (Haydock)

VERSE 33

Despised, or *the hated wife,* Deuteronomy xxi. 15. --- *Simeon,* "hearing or obedient."

VERSE 34

Levi, "adhesion or union." My husband will now stick to me.

VERSE 35

Juda, "praise or confession." (Calmet) --- *Left bearing* for a time. (Haydock) --- In the imposition of these names, Lia testified her gratitude to God. (Tirinus)

CHAPTER XXX

VERSE 1

Envied, or desired to have children like her. Thus we may envy the virtues of the saints. (Calmet) --- *Give me,* &c. These words seem to indicate a degree of impatience, at which we need not be surprised, when we reflect, that Rachel had been educated among idolaters. (Menochius) --- *Die* of grief and shame. "I shall be considered as one dead," Jun.[Junius] St. Chrysostom thinks she threatened to lay violent hands on herself, and through jealousy, spoke in a foolish manner. This passion is capable of the basest actions, (Haydock) and is almost unavoidable where polygamy reigns. (Calmet)

VERSE 2

Angry at the rash and apparently blasphemous demand of Rachel. (Menochius) --- *As God, pro Deo.* Am I to work a miracle in opposition to God, who has made thee barren? To him thou oughtest to address thyself. The Hebrews justly observe, that God has reserved to himself the four keys of nature: 1. Of generation; 2. Of sustenance, Psalm cxliv. 16;3. Of rain, Deuteronomy xxviii. 12; And, 4. Of the grave or resurrection, Ezechiel xxxvii. 12. (Tirinus)

VERSE 3

Servant, like a maid of honor. Josephus says she was not a slave, no more than Zelpha. --- *My knees,* whom I may nurse with pleasure. It was an ancient custom to place the newborn infants upon the knees of some near relation, who gave them a name, and thus in a manner adopted them. (chap. l. 22; Job iii. 12; Psalm xxi. 11) (Homer.) (Calmet)

VERSE 4

Marriage. The Manichees condemned Jacob for having more than four wives at once. But St. Augustine replied, it was not then unusual or forbidden. He took the two last only at the pressing instigation of Rachel and Lia, and that only for the sake of children. Lia herself was forced upon him. (contra Faust. xxii. 48.)

VERSE 6

Dan, means judgment. From the same root as Adonis; *Adoni,* my lord or judge, &c. Rachel's whole solicitude was for children. (Haydock)

VERSE 8

Compared me, &c. As Lia treacherously got my husband, so I have craftily surmounted the difficulties of barrenness; I have struggled earnestly, and have got the victory. *Patal,* means to act with cunning. (Psalm xvii. 27.) (Calmet) --- *Nephtali,* "a crafty wrestler." (Menochius)

VERSE 11

Happily, fortunately. --- *Gad,* or Bonaventure. (Haydock) ---"Good-fortune," was acknowledge by the pagans for a divinity; (Isaias lxv. 11.) perhaps for the Sun, or Oromagdes, the *Gad of Aram.* He was opposed to the wicked Arimenes in the Chaldean theology, by Zoroaster, (Calmet) the inventor of the Two Principles. Whether Lia intended to attribute this child to the influence of the planet Jupiter, the Sun, or some other tool, we cannot determine. (Haydock) --- Her naming may be simply; Behold I am now a mother of a troop, or little army, *Gad;* and to which (chap. xlix. 19.) Jacob evidently alludes. (Calmet)

VERSE 13

Aser: happy. My servant has now had as many sons as my sister (Menochius) and I have given them both names, indicating my great felicity and joy. (Haydock)

VERSE 14

Ruben, now perhaps about four years old, playing in the fields, in the latter *harvest* time, (Exodus ix. 32) *found mandrakes* of an extraordinary beauty and *flavor,* (Canticle of Canticles vii. 13.) whether they were flowers, lilies, jasmine, &c. as some translate; or rather, fruits of the mandrake tree, according to all the ancient versions; or of the citron, lemon, or orange tree, if we believe Calmet. *Dudaim* designates two breasts, or something lovely and protuberant. The ancients have spoken with admiration, and have attributed wonderful effects to the mandrakes, which, though controverted by moderns, might suffice to make Rachel greatly desire to have them; at least, if she believed they would contribute to remove her sterility, as Pliny, Natural History xxv. 15. Aristotle (de Gener. ii.) and other naturalists of eminence, have maintained they did. (Haydock) --- The effect which she desired so much, was not, however, to be attributed to them, since she conceived only three years after, and that by the blessing of God. (Tirinus)

VERSE 15

From me. Lia was aware that Jacob's affection lay entirely towards Rachel; particularly now, as she had ceased to bear children herself. (Haydock) --- *This might,* when it is my turn to have him. To prevent any jealousy, the husband visited his wives one after another, as was the case with Smerdis, the king of Persia. (Herodotus iii. 79; Exodus xxi. 10.) (Calmet)

VERSE 18

Issachar, "the reward of the man, *or* husband." (Calmet) --- She might allude also to the reward she had obtained for her mandrakes. (Haydock)

VERSE 20

Zabulon, "dwelling or cohabiting." Zobad (which resembles the sound of Zobal) means to endow, (Calmet) to which she seems also to refer; as if her marriage was renewed, and God had given her more children for a dowry. (Menochius)

VERSE 21

Dina, "judgment," like Dan. God hath done me justice. The Hebrews assert that Dina was married to holy Job. She was born the same year as Joseph, the 91st of Jacob. Lia brought forth seven children in seven years.

VERSE 24

Joseph. In imposing this name, Rachel looks both to the past and to the future; thanking God for *taking away* (asop) her reproach, and begging that He *would add* (isop or Joseph) the blessing of another son, as he really did, though it occasioned her death: so little do we know what we ask for! Joseph means one "adding or increasing," chap. xlix. 22. (Haydock) --- He was born when the 14 years of *service* were over; being a most glorious figure of Jesus Christ, who came to redeem us from slavery. (Du Hamel)

VERSE 28

Give thee. He wishes to engage him to continue in his service; being convinced, that a faithful and pious servant is a great treasure. Laban promises everything, and performs little according to his agreement. He never thinks of making Jacob any present for his extraordinary diligence.

VERSE 31

Nothing. I am willing to depart with my family towards my father. But if I must stay, these are my terms. (Haydock) --- I require no certain wages, committing myself entirely to what Providence shall send. (Salien.)

VERSE 32

Speckled; from those which are all of one color. Those which should be of the former description must belong to Jacob, while all the black and the white should be Laban's. --- *Brown,* or of a dull mixture of white and black. --- *Spotted,* having large patches of either color. --- *Divers,* little spots variegating the fleece. (Menochius) --- The original is extremely obscure. Jacob asks only for the worst; the speckled sheep and goats, also the black sheep and the white goats, ver. 35. (Bochart.) (Calmet)

VERSE 33

Of theft, if they be found in my possession. I am so well convinced that God will reward my justice, that, even contrary to what might naturally be expected, he will enable me to have plenty of spotted sheep and goats, though their mothers be all of one color. It is not certain, that Jacob agreed to have the flocks parted till the end of the year. (Menochius)

VERSE 35

His sons. These continued to observe the conduct of Jacob, while Laban drove off all the flocks of divers colors to so great a distance, ver. 36, that there was no danger of the sheep under Jacob's care getting to them. Thus Laban first began to violate the agreement; and the angel of the Lord suggested to Jacob, the plan by which he was preserved from serving a cruel and avaricious man without wages, chap. xxxi. 12. (Menochius)

VERSE 40

All the white, &c. Notwithstanding Jacob's stratagem, some had lambs all of a color. The force of fancy is very surprising on such occasions. Oppian, Aristotle, and others, recommend Jacob's plan as consonant to nature. (Haydock)

VERSE 42

Later-coming, in autumn, when the spring lambs were of an inferior value. These he was willing to abandon for the most part to Laban; and therefore did not use his rods. Pliny, Natural History viii. 47; and Columella viii. 3, agree, that the lambs which are produced in spring do not thrive so well as those of autumn, at least in Italy, and in those countries where sheep lamb twice a year. *Bis gravidæ pecudes,* Virgil. (Calmet) --- Many who have tried the same experiment as Jacob, have not experienced the same success; whence St. Chrysostom, and most of the Greek fathers, suppose that it was miraculous. (Tirinus)

CHAPTER XXXI
VERSE 1

After that six years were expired, and calumnies and ill-will attended Jacob in Laban's family, God ordered him to retire, ver. 3. (Haydock)

VERSE 7

Ten times. Very often, or perhaps this exact number of times, ver. 41.

VERSE 8

All, or the far greatest part, so that I was exceedingly enriched. (Menochius) --- The Septuagint here agrees with the Vulgate. But the Hebrew and other versions, instead of *white ones,* read *of divers colors,* or *ring-streaked,* which takes away th intended opposition. (Calmet)

VERSE 12

Of divers colors. Their fancy was strongly impressed with thee various colors, in consequence of the pilled rods, which they beheld: and which Jacob was directed by the angel to place in the troughs. --- *I have seen* with displeasure, the injustice of Laban; (Haydock) and therefore, I, the Lord of all things, authorize thee to act in this manner. By this vision, the justice of Jacob would appear; and the authority for removing, given in a second vision, would suffice to induce the two principal wives of Jacob to give their consent to leave their father's house, and to begin a long journey. During the last six years, Providence had given no increase of family, that the little children might be no impediment to the removal. (Haydock)

VERSE 15

Eaten up. Laban kept for himself the dowry paid by Jacob for his wives, though he ought to have allotted it to them, with the addition of something more, in proportion to his immense wealth. (Menochius)

VERSE 18

Gotten. Hebrew expresses over again, *the cattle of his getting,* &c., which is omitted in one manuscript, as well as in the Septuagint, Syriac, and Arabic versions, though yet used in the Samaritan copy. (Kennicott) --- *To Isaac,* who was still living, though he had apprehended death was at hand 20 years before. He continued to live other 20 years after. (Salien.) --- Jacob spent about 10 years at Sichem and at Bethel, before he went to dwell with Isaac. (Menochius)

VERSE 19

Her father's idols. By this it appears that Laban was an idolater: and some of the fathers are of opinion, that Rachel stole away these idols, to withdraw him from idolatry, by removing the occasion of his sin. (Challoner) --- Others think she was herself infected with this superstition, until Jacob entirely banished it from his family in Chanaan, chap. xxxv. 2. (Tirinus) --- The Hebrew *Teraphim,* is translated *images* by the Protestants in this place, though it certainly denotes idols. But Osee iii. 4, they leave it un-translated, lest they should be forced to allow that images pertain to religious service, as well as *sacrifice,* &c., which are mentioned together, (Worthington) though they now indeed have *images* in the same verse of Osee for what the Vulgate renders *altar.* These teraphims are consequently taken in a good as well as in a bad sense. They were, perhaps, made of rich metal, and taken by Rachel and Lia to indemnify them for the want of a dowry. This, however, was wrong, and done without the participation of their husband. (Haydock)

VERSE 20

Away. Hebrew, "Jacob stole the heart of Laban," concealing his flight from him. (Menochius)

The river Euphrates. --- *Galaad,* as it was called afterwards, ver. 48. (Menochius)

VERSE 22

Third day. He was gone to shear his sheep, distant three days' journey.

VERSE 24

Speak not. Laban did not comply exactly, but he used no violence. (Haydock)

VERSE 32

Slain. Homer says, "the father judges his children and wives;" and thus Jacob pronounces sentence. The Rabbins pretend it and its effect soon after in the death of Rachel, chap. xxxv. 18. (Calmet)

VERSE 35

Vain. For who would imagine, that a woman should treat in this manner the objects of her father's adoration? (Calmet) --- It would hence appear, that she did not herself adore them, unless fear overcame her religion. (Haydock)

VERSE 36

Angry. He was extremely quiet. But patience abused, turns to fury. (Menochius)

VERSE 39

Exact it. Laban acted in opposition both to custom and to justice, (Calmet) while Jacob forebore to claim what he might have done, agreeably to both. (Haydock)

VERSE 42

The fear of Isaac; or of that God, whom Isaac fears, on account of the danger to which he is exposed of losing his friendship; a thing which, Abraham being now departed in peace, has not to dread. (Calmet)

VERSE 43

Are mine, or proceed from me originally; so that if I were to injure them, I should disregard the dictates of nature. (Menochius)

VERSE 47

Testimony. Hebrew makes Laban give this etymology, *Jegar-saha-dutha;* while *Galaad* means the hill or the witness. The Syrian language had now begun to deviate some little from the Hebrew of Jacob. ---*Each,* &c. This is added by the Vulgate. (Calmet)

Behold. Hebrew, "and Mitspah," or "Hammitspah," the watch-tower, whence God will see us. (Calmet)

Over them. A wise precaution, which the rich Turks still observe when they give their daughters in marriage. (Busbeq. ep. 3.)

I have, &c. One Samaritan copy reads very properly, "thou hast set up," (*yarithi*), ver. 45. (Kennicott).

God of Nachor. Hebrew uses Elohim, which is often applied to idols, such as Nachor worshipped along with the true God. (Calmet) --- Jacob swears by the one only God, whom his father revered. (Menochius) --- *The God of their father* is omitted in the Septuagint and is deemed an interpolation by Kennicott. The Samaritan reads again *the God of Abraham.* (Haydock)

Night (*de nocte*) when it was just at an end, and day-light appeared. --- *His daughters,* with Dina, &c. Thus all ended well and in peace, by the divine interposition, after the most serious alarms. (Haydock)

CHAPTER XXXII
VERSE 1

Angels. Guardians of Chanaan and Mesopotamia. (Jarchi.) --- The latter escorted him as far as the torrent Jaboc. That angels guard different provinces, is well attested, Daniel xii. 1 and Acts xvi. 9. (Calmet) --- Michael protected Chanaan and the people of God. (Diodorus of Tarsus.) (Menochius)

VERSE 2

Mahanaim, "two camps." A town was afterwards built here.

VERSE 3

Edom; comprising the countries east, west, and south of the Dead sea. (Calmet) --- Providentially, Esau had now left his father's house open to his brother; who, on this occasion, addresses him with the utmost civility, and speaks of the riches which he had obtained; in order that Esau might neither be ashamed of him, nor suspect that he would impoverish his father. (Menochius)

VERSE 6

Men. Jonathan has *Polemarchoi;* officers or warriors, either to punish Jacob, (Wisdom x. 12.) as the latter feared, ver. 11; or to do him honor, as Esau protested, chap. xxxiii. 15. (Calmet)

VERSE 9

God of...Isaac. It is not true, therefore, that God never has the title of God of any man, while living, as some assert, chap. xxxi. 42. Jacob addresses him by those very titles which he had assumed at Bethel, chap. xxviii. 13. (Haydock)

VERSE 10

Not worthy. Chaldean, "my merits are beneath all thy kindnesses." St. Augustine reads, with St. Cyril, *idoneus es,* &c., "thou art sufficient for me."

VERSE 11

The children; sparing neither sex nor age, but destroying all. (Calmet) --- Jacob insists on the promises of God; yet fears lest he should, by some offence, have deserved to forfeit his protection; particularly, as he had been living 20 years among idolaters. He acts with all prudence. (Worthington)

VERSE 15

Camels. The milk of these animals is most exquisite, being mixed with three parts water. Pliny, Natural History xi. 41, who says, "They give milk till they be with young again." The Arabs feed chiefly on their milk and flesh. (St. Jerome, contra Jor. ii.) The value of all these presents, may give us some idea of the prodigious wealth which God had heaped upon Jacob in the space of six years! (Haydock)

VERSE 20

He said, &c. These words were not to be related to Esau; they are the words of the sacred historian. There were probably five droves of *goats, sheep, camels, kine and asses;* by the successive presenting of which, Esau might be appeased.

VERSE 22

Sons, with Dina his daughter, and all his household.

VERSE 23

All things. Grotius thinks this has been lost in the Hebrew copies; as it occurs in the Samaritan, Septuagint, and Syriac.

VERSE 24

A man, &c. This was an angel in human shape, as we learn from Osee xii. 4. He is called *God*, ver. 28 and 30, because he represented the person of the Son of God. This wrestling, in which Jacob, assisted by God, was a match for an angel, was so ordered, (ver. 28.) that he might learn by this experiment of the divine assistance, that neither Esau, nor any other man, should have power to hurt him. It was also spiritual, as appear by his earnest prayer, urging, and at last obtaining the angel's blessing. (Challoner) --- The father will not refuse a good gift to those who ask him with fervor and humility. Jacob had before set us an excellent pattern how to pray, placing his confidence in God, and distrusting himself, ver. 9, &c. (Haydock) --- It is not certain, whether Jacob remained *alone* on the northern or on the southern banks of Jaboc. (Calmet)

VERSE 25

Sinew, near the coxendix, or huckel-bone. (Du Hamel) This was to convince Jacob, how easily he could have gained the victory over him; and to make him remember, that it was not simply a vision, but a real wrestling. (Tirinus)

VERSE 28

Israel. This name was more honorable, and that by which his posterity were afterwards known; being called Israelites, and not Jacobites. God ratifies the title, chap. xxxv. 10. It means a prince of God, (St. Jerome, q. Heb.; Calmet) or one standing upright, and contending victoriously with God, *rectus Dei, yisrael.* (Haydock) --- Many have expounded it, *a man seeing God;* aiss-rae-al. (Philo, &c.)

VERSE 29

Why, &c. He represses Jacob's curiosity, (Haydock) perhaps because God did not as yet choose to reveal his name, Exodus vi. 3. Some Greek and Latin copies add, *which is wonderful,* taken from Judges xiii. 6, 18. (Calmet)

VERSE 30

Phanuel. This word signifies *the face of God,* or *the sight,* or *seeing of God.* (Challoner) --- Hebrew reads here Peni-el, though it has Phanuel in the next verse. Jacob thus returns thanks to God for the preservation of his life, after having seen God or his angel in a corporeal form, and not in a dream only. (Calmet)

VERSE 31

Halted, or was lame. Alulensis thinks the angel healed him very soon. (Menochius)

VERSE 32

The sinew in beasts of any kind, corresponding with that part of *Jacob's thigh.* (Haydock) --- Some refrain from the whole quarter, others extract the sinew. This they do, without any command, in memory of this transaction. (Calmet)

CHAPTER XXXIII
VERSE 3

Forward, before his family; like a good father, exposing himself to the greatest danger. (Menochius) --- *Seven times,* to testify his great humility and respect for his brother. How, then, can anyone find fault with Catholics, if they bow down before the cross thrice on Good Friday, to testify their great veneration for their expiring Lord?

VERSE 8

Favor. Esau had already heard from the servants. But he asks again, meaning to excuse himself from receiving them. (Haydock) --- This civil and unexpected behavior, filled the breast of Jacob with such gratitude and love, that he made use of an hyperbole, *I have seen,* &c. *of God.* Chaldean, "of a prince," Syriac, "of an angel," Elohim. See 2 Kings xix. 27; Esther xv. 16. (Calmet) --- *A little present.* Hebrew *monee,* or *mincha,* calculated to shew the subjection of the giver. (Menochius)

VERSE 13

Young, boves fœtus, giving milk, having calved lately, Septuagint. (Bochart.) (Calmet)

VERSE 14

In Seir; not immediately, but as soon as it might be convenient. This time perhaps never arrived. (St. Augustine, q. 106.)

VERSE 18

The town of Salem, which was the first town of Chanaan that he came near after his return. It was afterwards called Sichem, and Sichar, John iv. 5, and Naplosa. *Salim,* mentioned John iii. 23, was probably more to the east. Some translate, "He came quite *sound* to the city of Sichem;" where, Demetrius says, he dwelt ten years, Eusebius, præp. ix. 21, having stopped at Socoth six months. (Calmet) --- This seems very probable, as Dina met with her misfortune a little before he left the country; and as she was six years old when she came from Haran, she would be about 15 when she began to go a visiting, &c., chap. xxxiv. 1. (Haydock)

VERSE 19

Lambs. Hebrew, Kossite, or Kesita, a word which occurs also, Josue xxvi. 32, and Job xlii. 11; and may signify lambs, or a species of money, marked perhaps with their figure. It may also denote pearls, coral, a vessel, or purse of *good* money. St. Stephen, Acts vii. 19, mentions the *price of money.* But he probably speaks of the bargain made by Abraham with Ephron, son of Heth, for which some have substituted Hemor, the son of Sichem. Kista in the Chaldean means a vessel or measure; and we learn from Herodotus iii. 130, that the Persians were accustomed to keep their money in this manner. In the Chaldean, Syriac, and Arabic languages, there are words derived from the same root as Kesita, which mean purity, perfection; and thus what Jacob gave was good current money; (Calmet) or such things as we received among merchants.

VERSE 20

The most, &c. El Elohe Yisrael. By this name he dignified the altar, consecrating his field and all his possessions to God, and acknowledging that all was his gift. (Haydock)

CHAPTER XXXIV

VERSE 1

Country, when a great festival was celebrated. (Josephus, Antiquities i. 18.) Dina was urged by curiosity to see and to be seen. Let others take example from her, and beware of associating with infidels, and of opening their hearts to pleasure at fairs and nocturnal meetings.

VERSE 2

Virgin. Hebrew and Septuagint, "He humbled *or* afflicted the virgin." It is well if she made all the resistance she was able, and resented the indignity; as she seems to have done, though Sichem tried all means to comfort her. (Haydock)

VERSE 5

Heard this, perhaps, from Dina's companion. (Menochius)

VERSE 7

In Israel, or against the honor and peace of their father and all his family. --- *An unlawful act*, which some nevertheless commit without scruple, and even dare to represent as a matter of small consequence if they marry afterwards!

VERSE 10

Command, or you are at liberty to purchase and *till* it as you please. (Haydock)

VERSE 12

Dowry for Dina. --- *Gifts* for her parents and brothers, chap. xxiv. 53. (Calmet)

VERSE 13

Deceitfully. The sons of Jacob, on this occasion, were guilty of a grievous sin, as well by falsely pretending religion, as by excess of their revenge. Though, otherwise their zeal against so foul a crime was commendable. (Challoner) --- In this light it is viewed by Judith ix. 2. Simeon and Levi spoke on this occasion, Septuagint, as they were afterwards the chief actors, ver. 25. There were commissioned by their father to speak for him; but Jacob was ignorant of their deceit. (Haydock)

VERSE 14

Abominable. To be uncircumcised, was a reproach among the Hebrews. Yet there was no law forbidding to marry such. Laban was of this description, and the Chanaanites also; whose daughters the sons of Jacob themselves espoused, at least Juda and this very Simeon, as the Scripture assures us.

VERSE 17

Daughter, the only one of our father; who, it would hence appear, was detained by Hemor, ver. 26. (Calmet)

VERSE 19

The greatest man, (inclytus) perhaps associated to his father in the government of the town. Yet he is willing to submit to this painful operation. (Haydock)

VERSE 20

Gate. Here judgment was given, the markets held, &c. They endeavored to convince the *people,* that the conditions offered would be for their interest. (Menochius)

VERSE 23

Ours, by mutual commerce. The Rabbin pretend the Sichemite designed to circumvent Jacob and his family. But their conduct seems to screen them from any reproach of this kind, and Jacob throws the blame upon his own sons, chap. xlix. 6. If Hemor said more than he was authorized by them to do, this will not palliate their injustice and sacrilegious perfidy. (Calmet) (Menochius)

VERSE 25

Greatest. On that day a fever and inflammation likewise often take place. See Hippocrates on fractures, Valesius sac. (Phil. xii.) (Menochius) --- *Brothers of Dina* by Lia, and both of a fiery temper. They were assisted by some servants, (Menochius) and afterwards the other children helped to pillage the city. (Theodotion, ap. Eusebius, ix. 22.)

VERSE 29

Captive. No doubt Jacob would force them to restore such ill-gotten goods. (Calmet) --- They had acted without authority, and even contrary to the known disposition of their father. They rashly exposed him to destruction, which would inevitably have taken place, if God had not protected him, chap. xxxv. 5. (Haydock)

VERSE 31

Should they, &c. This answer, full of insolence, to a father who was as much hurt by the indignity offered to Dina as they could be, heightens their crime. Sichem was the only one among the citizens really guilty, unless perhaps some of his servants might have given him assistance; and Hemor, the king, might contract some stain by not causing a better police to be observed, and by not punishing his son with greater severity, and not sending Dina home, &c. But why are the harmless citizens to be involved in ruin? unless *Quicquid delirant Reges, plectuntur Achivi.* (Haydock)

Procopius says Hemor also abused Dina; but the plural is here used for the singular, and this author builds upon a false supposition. Calmet)

CHAPTER XXXV

VERSE 1

God dissipates Jacob's well-grounded fears, and sends him to perform his vow, chap. xviii. 13. (Haydock)

VERSE 2

Strange gods, which his servants had reserved in the plundering of Sichem; perhaps he had also been informed of Rachel's theft. (Du Hamel) ---*Garments;* put on your cleanest and best attire, to testify the purity with which you ought to approach to the service of God. (Menochius) --- See Exodus xix. 10; Leviticus xv. 13.

VERSE 4

And the ear-rings. Hebrew, hanezamim; such as had been consecrated to some idol, and adorned the ears of those false but gaudy deities. (Menochius) --- Men and women used them likewise, as phylacteries or talismans, to which many superstitious virtues were attributed. (St. Augustine, ep. 73, ad Posid. 9, iii. in Gen.; Ezechiel xvi. 12; Proverbs xxv.; Exodus xxxv.; Judges viii. (Calmet) --- *The turpentine tree;* or "an oak tree," as the Hebrew *haela* means also. Septuagint adds, "and he destroyed them till this present day;" which seems intended to refute the story of their being found and adored by the Samaritans, or employed by Solomon when he built the temple. Jacob buried them privately. (Calmet) See Deuteronomy vii. 5.

VERSE 5

Terror of God. A panic fear, which the pagans thought was sent by Pan. (Calmet) --- God can easily make the most powerful flee before a few. St. Augustine, q. 112.

VERSE 6

Chanaan, to distinguish it from another. Judges i. 26, (Menochius) or because Moses wrote this in Arabia. (Calmet)

VERSE 7

To him. Hebrew literally, "He called that place the God of Bethel, because there God (*or* the angels) appeared to him." *Haelohim,* with a verb plural, generally refers to angels; when it is applied to God, the article is omitted, and the verb is singular. (Calmet)

VERSE 8

Debora. The Rabbin say she had been sent to urge Jacob's return. (Menochius) --- Perhaps she was come to see him and the daughters of Laban, for whom she would naturally have a great regard, as she lived with Laban. --- *Weeping.* This shows the great respect they had for this good old servant. (Haydock)

VERSE 10

Israel. This name signifies one that prevail with God; (Challoner) and is more honorable and expressive than that of Jacob. God confirms what had been declared by his angel, chap. xxxii. 28.

VERSE 12

And to, &c. *And* is often put by way of explanation. Chanaan was possessed by all the twelve sons of Jacob. Those of the handmaids are not excluded, as Ismael had been. (Worthington)

VERSE 14

Set up either a fresh altar, or restored the stone which he had formerly used for sacrifice. (St. Augustine q. 116.) --- *Drink,* wine. --- *Oil.* Theophrastus, speaking of a man addicted to superstition, says, "he adores every anointed stone." (Calmet)

VERSE 16

Spring. Hebrew, cibrath. Septuagint leave it un-translated, Chalratha, though they render it horse-race, (ver. 19) and join both together, chap. xlviii. 7. The word occurs again, 4 Kings v. 19; and St. Jerome translates it the spring, or the finest time of the earth. Others suppose it signifies the high road, (ver. 19) or horse-course, or a mile, &c. as if the place, where Rachel died, and not the season of the year, were designated. Calmet concludes, she died about the distance of an acre (*sillon,* furrow or ridge) from Ephrata. But there seems to be no reason why we should recede from the Vulgate. (Haydock)

VERSE 18

That is. These etymologies are given by St. Jerome. (Du Hamel) --- *Right hand, (jemini)* as he is often styled in Scripture. *Jamin* has the same meaning; though it may also signify *of the south,* with respect to Bethel and Sichem; or *of days and old age,* chap. xliv. 20. 1. (Calmet) Jacob chooses to give his son a more auspicious name; as the other would have reminded him too sensibly of his loss. (Haydock)

VERSE 20

A pillar; or sepulchral monument, about 500 paces north of Bethlehem, (Haydock) which was called Ephrata afterwards, from Caleb's wife. (Calmet)

VERSE 21

Tower. Hebrew, Heder, about a mile to the east of Bethlehem, where the angels appeared to announce the birth of Christ. St. Helen built a temple there in honor of the angels. (Tirinus) ---

Shepherds had such places to keep watch. (Calmet) --- There was a tower of this name near Jerusalem. (Micheas iv. 8; St. Jerome, q. His.)

The concubine. She was his lawful wife; but according to the style of the Hebrews, is called *concubine,* because of her servile extraction. (Challoner) --- *Ignorant of:* and therefore, to mark his displeasure, he deprived him of the birth-right, chap. xlix. 4. Jacob approached no more to Bala, as David had no farther commerce with the wives whom Absalom had defiled, 2 Kings xvi. 22. (Menochius) --- The Septuagint add, *and it appeared evil in his sight;* an omission which the Hebrew editions seem to acknowledge, by leaving a vacant space. (Kennicott)

Syria, all except Benjamin. (Calmet) --- *All* frequently means the greatest part. (Haydock)

Spent. He lived 42 years, after he had blessed Jacob. --- *His people,* in the bosom of Abraham, in limbo. --- *Full of days,* quite satisfied. *Cedat uti conviva satur.* (Hor.[Horace] Sat. i. 1.) He was one of the brightest figures of Jesus Christ, on account of him miraculous birth, name, willingness to be sacrificed, marriage with a woman sought at a great distance, &c. (Calmet) --- *Esau,* who had always shown a great regard for his father, joins his brother in rendering to him the last rites of burial. (Haydock) --- Rebecca was probably dead. (Menochius) --- The death of Isaac is mentioned out of its place, that the history of Joseph may not be interrupted, as it happened when Joseph was in prison, in the year of the world 2288. (Calmet)

CHAPTER XXXVI
VERSE 1

Edom. His genealogy extends as far as ver. 20, where that of Seir, the Horrite, begins. The seven first verses specify Esau's sons, the twelve next his grandsons born in Seir. From the 15th to the 20th verse, we have the most ancient form of government in that nation under the *Aluphim,* or heads of families. To them succeed *kings,* (ver. 31 to 40) and then *dukes* to the end. Moses omits several generations of Oolibama's grand-children, as foreign to his purpose, which was to show the Israelites whom they were not to molest. The *kings,* of whom he speaks, (ver. 31) might govern different parts of the country at the same time; and that before any form of government was established among the Hebrews, as it was under Moses, who is styled a king, (Deuteronomy xxxiii. 5) about 200 years after Esau had driven the Horrites from their mountains. (Calmet) --- Among these nations several good men might exist, as Job, &c. But the true religion was preserved more fully among the 12 tribes. (St. Augustine, City of God xv. xvi.) (Worthington)

VERSE 2

Ada. These wives of Esau are called by other names, chap. xxvi. But it was very common amongst the ancients for the same persons to have two names, as Esau himself was also called Edom. (Challoner) --- *Ana, the daughter of Sebeon.* It is not certain that Ana was a woman. The Samaritan and Septuagint make him son of Sebeon, both here and ver. 14, (Haydock) as well as some Latin copies; and he is mentioned as such, ver. 24. The *daughter* of Sebeon may, therefore, designate his grand-daughter, which is not unusual. Sebeon is called *Hevite, Hethite,* and *Horrite,* on account of his dwelling in different countries; though some think they were different persons. (Calmet) --- This, and innumerable other difficulties, may convince Protestants that the Scriptures are not easy. (Worthington)

VERSE 4

Eliphaz; perhaps the Themanite, and friend of Job, (St. Jerome) or his grandfather, by Theman; as Job was the grandson of Esau, and the second king, ver. 33. (Tirinus)

VERSE 6

Jacob, by the divine Providence, as Chanaan was to be his inheritance. (Menochius) --- He had returned from Seir about the same time as Jacob came home. (St. Augustine, q. 119.)

VERSE 9

Of Edom, or of all the nations who inhabited Idumea, sprung from Esau's grand-children. (Calmet)

VERSE 15

Aluph, prince of a tribe, or of a thousand; a Chiliarch. Zach. v. 2 [Zacharias v. 2]. The Rabbin assert they wore not a crown, as the kings did. (Calmet) --- Both obtained their authority by election. An aristocracy prevailed under the dukes. (Menochius)

VERSE 16

Duke Core, being the son of Esau, is omitted in the Samaritan though found in all the versions and Hebrew. (Kennicott)

VERSE 24

Hot waters. Medicinal, (Menochius) like the springs at Bath, &c. (Haydock) --- Hebrew *hayemim,* a word which some translate *mules;* others, the nation of that name; or the giants, *Emeans,* with whom he had perhaps some engagement, as Adad (ver. 35) had with the Madianites, the particulars of which were then well known. The Septuagint and ancient versions retain the original word. It is used for a body of water. (Calmet)

VERSE 30

Seir, contemporary with the princes of Esau, in another town or region. (Calmet)

VERSE 31

A king. See ver. 1. Moses might also add this with reference to the times, when he knew the Hebrews would petition for a king, for whom he gave particular laws. (Menochius) --- These kings were probably foreigners, who subdued the natives. They did not obtain the kingdom by succession. (Calmet)

VERSE 33

Jobab. Most people suppose this is Job, the model of patience. (Menochius) --- *Bosra,* or *Bezer,* was the capital of Idumea, in the tribe of Ruben. (Calmet)

VERSE 37

River Rohoboth; or as it is expressed, 1 Paralipomenon i. 48, *of Rohoboth, which is near the river* Euphrates, below where the Chaboras empties itself.

VERSE 38

Adar. Many confound him with the king, whom David overcame. --- *Daughter of Mezaab,* or perhaps her grand-daughter, or adopted child.

VERSE 40

Callings. They left their names to various places. They were in power when the Hebrews approached their respective territories, and threw them into dismay, Exodus xv. 15. --- *Alva.* Septuagint, gola. (Calmet)

VERSE 43

The same Edom *is Esau.* Moses seems particularly attentive to assert both titles for the same person, ver. 8, &c. The time of Esau's death cannot be ascertained. There is reason to hope that he died penitent; though in the early part of his life, he gave way to his ferocious temper, and became a figure of the reprobate. He lived on terms of friendship with his brother, assisted him to bury his father, &c. (Calmet) --- He was a hunter, indeed; which St. Jerome looks upon as a bad sign: "nunquam venatorem in bonam partem legi," in Micheas v. But this was also in his younger days. (Haydock) --- *I have hated Esau,* Matthew i., refers to his irreligious posterity, and to his being deprived of temporal advantages, attending the birth-right. (Tirinus) (Calmet)

CHAPTER XXXVII
VERSE 1

Sojourned at Hebron and the environs. (Haydock)

VERSE 2

Generations. This connects his history with chap. xxxv. What happened to Jacob and his sons, and particularly to Joseph, forms the subject of the remaining part of Genesis. (Haydock) --- *Old;* complete, or beginning "his 17th year," as the Hebrew, Chaldean, and Septuagint have it. "He was the son or boy of"---so many years always means the current year unfinished. (Bochart 1. R. xiii. 1.) --- *The sons.* Perhaps these were not so much enraged against Joseph, till he told his father of their scandalous behavior, in order that he might put a stop to it. --- *He accused.* Some editions of the Septuagint read, "they accused him," &c.; but all others confirm the Vulgate and Hebrew. (Calmet) --- *Crime:* perhaps of sodomy, or bestiality (St. Thomas Aquinas); or of abusive language to Joseph himself. (Calmet)

VERSE 3

Old age, and therefore expected to have no more children; but he loved him still more, on account of his innocent and sweet behavior (Menochius): in which sense the Samaritan,

Chaldean, &c., have, "because he was a wise and prudent boy." --- *Colors.* The nations of the East delight in gaudy attire, "hanging down to the heels" as the original *passim* is sometimes expressed, *talaris & polymita,* ver. 3. (Calmet)

VERSE 4

Could not, through envy, which caused them to notice every little distinction shown to Joseph. They perceived he was the most beloved. His accusing them, and insinuating by his mysterious dreams that he would be their lord, heightened their rage. (Haydock)

VERSE 5

A dream. These dreams of Joseph were *prophetical,* and sent from God, as were also those which he interpreted, chap. xl and xli; otherwise, generally speaking, the observing of dreams is condemned in the Scripture, as superstitious and sinful. See Deuteronomy xviii. 10 and Ecclesiasticus xxxiv. 2, 3.

VERSE 7

Sheaf. Joseph probably knew not what this portended, as the prophets were sometimes ignorant of the real purport of their visions. (Calmet) --- But it admirably foreshowed the famine, which would bring his brethren to adore him in Egypt. (Menochius)

VERSE 9

The sun. This second dream confirmed the truth of the former. Joseph relates it with simplicity, not suspecting the ill will of his brethren: but his father easily perceives what effect the narration would have, and desires him to be more cautious. He even points out the apparent incoherence of the dream, as Rachel, who seemed intended by the *moon,* was already dead; unless this dream happened before that event. St. Augustine (q. 123) observes, this was never literally verified in Joseph, but it was in Jesus Christ, whom he prefigured. (Calmet) --- Some think that Bala, the nurse of Joseph, was intended by the moon. (Tirinus)

VERSE 10

Worship. This word is not used here to signify *divine worship,* but an *inferior veneration,* expressed by the bowing of the body, and that, according to the manner of the eastern nations, down to the ground.

VERSE 11

With himself not doubting but it was prophetical. Thus acted the Blessed Virgin. (Calmet)

VERSE 13

In Sichem. About ninety miles off. The town had not probably been as yet rebuilt. Jacob had a field there, and the country was free for anyone to feed their flocks. It was customary to drive them to a distance. (Calmet)

VERSE 14

Bring me. He was afraid of letting him remain with them, and retained him mostly at home for company, and to protect him from danger.

VERSE 16

My brethren. The man was acquainted with Jacob's family, as he had dwelt in those parts for a long time. (Haydock)

VERSE 17

Dothain: twelve miles to the north of Samaria. (Eusebius)

VERSE 19

The dreamer. Hebrew *Bahal hachalomoth,* "the lord of dreams," or the visionary lord (Calmet); or one who feigns dreams: so the Jews say of our Savior, *this seducer.* (Haydock)

VERSE 20

Pit: walled around to contain water: Hebrew *Bur. Bar* means a well that has no walls. (Menochius) --- *Shall appear.* They resolve to tell a lie, and easily believe that Joseph had been as bad as themselves in telling one first. If they had believed the dreams were from God, they would hardly have supposed that they could prevent them from having their effect. (Haydock)

VERSE 22

His father. Ruben wished to regain his father's favor, chap. xxxv. 22.

VERSE 25

To eat bread. How could they do this while their innocent brother was praying and lamenting! (chap. xlii. 21.) (Haydock) --- *Some:* a caravan of merchants. (Du Hamel) --- *Balm,* or rosin; "That of Syria resembles attic honey." (Pliny, Natural History) --- *Myrrh,* (stacten); Hebrew, *Lot:* "drops of myrrh or laudanum, or of the Lotus tree." (Calmet)

VERSE 28

Of silver. Some have read, thirty pieces of gold or silver. (St. Ambrose, c. 3.) --- The price was trifling: twenty sides would be about £2 5s. 7½d. English. The Madianites and Ismaelites jointly purchased Joseph. (Haydock)

VERSE 29

Ruben, who, in the mean time had been absent while his brethren hearkened to the proposal of Juda only, and therefore consented to this evil. (Haydock)

VERSE 30

I go to seek for him. His brethren inform him of what they had done, and he consents to keep it a secret from his father. (Menochius)

VERSE 33

A beast. So he might reasonably conclude from the blood, and from the insinuations of the messengers sent by his ten sons, (Haydock) whom he would not suspect of so heinous a crime. Wild beasts infested that country. (Menochius)

VERSE 34

Sack-cloth, or hair-cloth, *cilicio.* These garments were made very close, like a sack, of the hair taken from the goats of Cilicia, which grew long, rough, and of a dark color. The poorest people used them:*Usum in Castrorum & miseris velamina nautis,* (Vir.[Virgil] Geor. 3); and the Ascetics, or monks, afterwards chose them for the sake of mortification and humility. (Calmet) --- Jacob was the first, mentioned in Scripture, who put them on, and the Israelites imitated him in their mourning. --- *Long time;* twenty-three years, till he heard of his son being still alive. (Menochius)

VERSE 35

Into hell; that is, into *limbo,* the place where the souls of the just were received before the death of our Redeemer. For allowing that the word *hell* sometimes is taken for the *grave,* it cannot be so taken in this place; since Jacob did not believe his son to be in the *grave,* (whom he supposed to be devoured by a wild beast) and therefore could not mean to go down to him thither: but certainly meant the place of rest, where he believed his soul to be. (Challoner) --- *Soal,* or sheol, *to crave,* denotes the receptacle of the dead, (Leigh) or a lower region; the grave for the body; *limbo,* or *hell,* when speaking of the soul. See Delrio, Adag. in 2 Kings, p. 209. (Haydock) --- Protestants here translate it, "the grave," being unwilling to admit a third place in the other world for the soul. See the contrary in St. Augustine, ep. 99, ad Evod; City of God xx. 15. (Worthington)

VERSE 36

An eunuch. This word sometimes signifies a *chamberlain, courtier,* or *officer* of the king: and so it is taken in this place. (Challoner) --- *Soldiers,* cooks, or butchers. Hebrew *tabachim,* executioners,*mactantium.* He might also be chief sacrificer, governor of the prisons, &c., all these employments were anciently very honorable, Daniel ii. 14. The providence of God never shines more brightly in any part of the Scripture, than in this history of Joseph, except in that of Jesus Christ, of whom Joseph was a beautiful figure. He was born when his father was grown old, as Jesus was in the last age of the world; he was *a son increasing,* as Jesus *waxed in age and grace before God and men;* both were beloved by their father, both comely, &c. (Calmet)

CHAPTER XXXVIII
VERSE 1

At that time Juda, twenty years old, marries the daughter of Sue, and has three sons by her during the three following years. The first takes Thamar to wife, when he was seventeen. Onan marries her the next year; after which she remains a widow about three years, when she bears twins to Juda. Phares goes down with him into Egypt, and has children there during Jacob's life. On this account, they are numbered among those who went down with Jacob, (chap. xlvi. 12) as the children of Benjamin seem to be likewise. Thus all these events might happen during the twenty-three years that Jacob dwelt in Chanaan, and the seventeen that he sojourned in Egypt. Some have thought the time too short, and have concluded that Juda had been married long before Joseph's slavery. He was, however, only four years older. (Calmet)

VERSE 5

Sela. Juda gave the name of Her to his first-born, as the Hebrew shows. His wife gave names to the two latter. --- *Ceased;* Hebrew *casbi:* "she died in bearing him," as Aquila has it. Most commentators take the word for the name of a place mentioned, Josue xv. 44. "He (Juda) was at Casbi when she bare him."

VERSE 7

Wicked; without shame or remorse, sinning against nature, in order, if we may believe the Jews, that the beauty of his wife might not be impaired by having children. Onan was actuated by envy. (Menochius)

VERSE 8

Wife. This was then customary among the Chanaanites, as Philo insinuates. It also continued to be practiced in Egypt, till the year of Christ 491 at least, when the marriage had not been consummated. Moses established it as a law, when no issue had sprung from the deceased brother. (Calmet) (Deuteronomy xxv. 5.) The eldest son bore his name; the rest were called after their own father. This law is now abrogated; and the prohibition, which has been issued by the Church, can be dispensed with only by herself, (Worthington) as was the case in the marriage of Henry VIII, with Catherine, the virgin relict of his brother Arthur. (Haydock)

VERSE 10

Slew him, perhaps by the hand *of evil angels,* Psalm lxxvii. 49. Asmodeus, &c., who slew the libidinous husbands of Sara. (Tobias iii. 7.) (Menochius) --- If an exemplary vengeance were oftener taken of the perpetrators of such a *detestable thing,* this abominable and unnatural vice would sooner perhaps be eradicated. (Haydock)

VERSE 11

Till. Juda had no design to give her to Sela, as the custom of that age required. (Calmet) --- She waited patiently for a time; when, perceiving that she was neglected, she devised a wicked scheme to punish Juda, even at the hazard of her own life. (Haydock)

VERSE 14

Veil; (theristrum) a long robe, covering the whole body, except the eyes. Thus she was *disguised;* or, as it were, masked, as Aquila translates. Harlots herein imitated modest women, chap. xxiv. 65. --- *Cross way.* Hebrew *Henayim,* which the Septuagint and Syriac take for a proper name. Others translate "at the gate of the eyes," which means two roads, where a person must open his eyes to judge which is the right one---or "at the gate of the two fountains leading to Thamnas," Judges xiv. 1. Prostitutes formerly infested the high roads. (Jeremias iii. 2; Ezechiel xvi. 25.) Chrysippus says, "at first harlots remained out of the city, and covered their faces; but afterwards growing more hardened, they laid aside the mask," &c.

VERSE 18

Staff. These were all marks of dignity. "Kings made use of spears, or scepters, before they wore a diadem." (Trogus. 43.) (Calmet) --- Juda might blame himself for exposing these valuable things, and divesting himself of all his dignity, to gratify his unjustifiable passion. If some have excused both the parties concerned, the Scripture at least sufficiently shows in what light we ought to consider their conduct. Juda himself thought her worthy of death; though in some sense, she was *juster* than himself, ver. 24, 26. (Haydock) --- She was guilty of a sort of adultery, being engaged to Sela; and also of incest, &c.; whereas the fault of Juda, through ignorance of her person, was simply fornication; which is, however, always contrary to the law of nature, as the pagans themselves confessed. (Grotius in Matthew v.) (Calmet) --- From Christ's choosing to be born of such progenitors, we may learn to adore his humility and tender regard for sinners. (Haydock)

VERSE 21

Harlot. Hebrew *Kedesha* a person *consecrated* to good or evil. Many nations esteemed prostitution, in honor of Venus, as a laudable action, 2 Kings xvii. 30. (Calmet)

VERSE 23

Lie. Hebrew, "lest we be exposed to shame," by making any farther search. (Menochius)

VERSE 25

Execution. The Rabbin say she was to be marked with a hot iron. If she was to die, before she was delivered, God prevented the cruel sentence from taking effect. (Haydock) --- Many nations have punished adultery with fire. Macrinus, the Roman emperor, ordered the culprits to be tied together and thrown into the flames. (Capitolin) --- Moses commanded the daughters of priests, who should be detected in this crime, to be given to the flames, (Leviticus xxi. 9,) and others to be stoned; (Leviticus xx. 10) whence the Rabbin have concluded, that Thamar was a priest's daughter. (Calmet)

VERSE 26

Juster. For Juda had been guilty of injustice; and had thus exposed her to the danger of following a life of lewdness. (Haydock) --- She remained a widow afterwards, as she was now rendered unfit to be married either to Juda or Sela. The latter married another woman, Numbers xxvi. 19. (Calmet) --- While Juda was engaged in this unlawful commerce, and yielded to the temptation, Joseph was triumphing over a much greater temptation, in rejecting the solicitations of his master's wife. (Haydock)

VERSE 29

Partition; the *secundinæ.* The midwife was apprehensive of danger. (Menochius) --- *Phares.* That is, a breach or division. (Challoner)

VERSE 30

Zara. "Orient, or rising;" in whose hand the red ribbon denoted, that the blood of Christ is the source of all our merits and happiness. These two brothers were a type of the vocation of the Gentiles, and of the reprobation of the Jews, who lost the privileges to which they thought themselves entitled. (St. Irenæus iv. 42; St. Chrysostom; &c.) (Calmet) --- Phares was the ancestor of Jesus Christ, St. Matthew i. 3.

CHAPTER XXXIX
VERSE 1

Ismaelites. They are called Madianites, chap. xxxvii. 36. (Haydock)

VERSE 6

Bread. A proverbial expression, to show how entirely he reposed in Joseph's fidelity and prudence. (Menochius) --- He was so rich, that he knew not the extent of his wealth. So Petronius says, *Nescit quid habeat, adeo Zaplutus est.* It may also be understood as a commendation of Joseph's disinterestedness.

VERSE 7

Many days. About 10 years; as Joseph was 30, three years after this. (Calmet)

VERSE 9

His wife, and such things as could not be touched without sin; such as his daughter, if the woman, whom Joseph afterwards married, was the daughter of this man, chap. xli. 45. --- *My God,* Elohim; which might also be understood of his lord and master. The sin against the latter would be resented by God, who is offended by every transgression. (Haydock)

VERSE 10

Both the woman was importunate, &c. Hebrew does not express this so fully. (Du Hamel)

VERSE 12

Out. He could easily have wrested it from her. But he would not do anything that might seem disrespectful, nor claim what her impure hands had touched. (Menochius)

VERSE 16

A proof of her fidelity, or *an argument to gain credit, argumentum fidei.* (Challoner) --- Love neglected, turns to fury. She wishes to take away Joseph's life, according to the laws of Egypt against adulterers. Diodorus says Sesostris burnt some women taken in the crime; and we must attribute it to divine Providence, that the enraged husband did not inflict instant death upon his slave. Perhaps he did not altogether believe him guilty. (Haydock)

VERSE 17

Thou hast, &c. As if her husband were guilty of an indiscretion. (Menochius)

VERSE 19

Too much. The proof was of an ambiguous nature. But Putiphar perhaps thought it unbecoming to distrust his wife, or to interrogate his slave. (Haydock)

VERSE 21

Keeper. Pererius thinks this was the same Putiphar, who, recognizing the innocence of Joseph, allows him every indulgence in prison; but does not liberate him, for fear of the dishonor and resentment of his wife. (Calmet) --- He had before put him in *irons.* (Psalm civ. 18; Wisdom x. 13.) Joseph here exercises at once the four cardinal virtues. *Prudence,* in keeping out of the company of his mistress, as the Hebrew express it, ver. 10: "He yielded not to lie with her, or to be in her company." (Haydock) --- *Justice,* in regard to his master. *Fortitude,* in bearing with all sorts of hardships, loss of character, &c. And *Temperance,* by refusing to gratify the most violent of all passions, at an age when it is the most insidious and ungovernable. This makes the fathers exclaim, we wonder more at the conduct of Joseph, than at the delivery of the three children from the Babylonian furnace. [Daniel iii.] For, like them, Joseph continues unhurt, and more shining in the midst of the flames. (St. Chrysostom) (Tirinus) --- The stories of Hippolitus, Bellerophon, &c., seem to be copied from this. (Calmet)

CHAPTER XL

VERSE 1

Two eunuchs; chief officers, and high in dignity, as the Hebrew expresses it, ver. 2. (Haydock) --- *Offended,* perhaps, by stealing, or by some treasonable conspiracy. (Menochius)

VERSE 2

And, &c. Hebrew, "Pharao was enraged against two of his officers; against the chief of the butlers," &c. *Mashkim.* St. Jerome translates this word *procurator domus,* "steward of the house," chap. xv. 2. No slave was entrusted with these high offices in the courts of Egypt and of Persia.

VERSE 3

Commander. Putiphar. (Calmet) --- *Prisoner,* though his chains were struck off. (Menochius)

VERSE 5

According to, &c. foreshowing what would happen to them, as Joseph afterwards interpreted the dreams. (Tirinus)

VERSE 8

Doth not interpretation belong to God? When dreams are from God, as these were, the interpretation of them is a gift of God. But the generality of dreams are not of this sort; but either proceed from the natural complexions and dispositions of persons, or the roving of their imaginations in the day on such objects as they are much affected with, or from their mind being disturbed with cares and troubles, and oppressed with bodily infirmities: or they are suggested by evil spirits, to flatter, or to terrify weak minds; in order to gain belief, and so draw them into error or superstition; or at least to trouble them in their sleep, whom they cannot move while they are awake: so that the general rule, with regard to dreams, is not to observe them, nor to give any credit to them. (Challoner) --- Physicians indeed, sometimes from some judgment of the nature of a distemper from dreams; on which subject, Hippocrates and Galen have written. But to pretend to discover by them the future actions of free agents, would be superstitious, Deuteronomy xviii. 10. (Tirinus) --- Justin (xxxvi. 2,) says, "Joseph was the first interpreter of dreams, and often gave proofs of his knowledge," &c.

VERSE 14

Prison, after examining into the justice of my cause.

VERSE 15

Hebrews. Chanaan, a *foreign* land with respect to Egypt, as was also Mesopotamia, where he was born. (Haydock) --- Joseph only maintains his own innocence, without accusing any one. (Menochius)

VERSE 16

Of meal. Hebrew may also mean "white, full of holes," &c.

VERSE 19

From thee, by decapitation. This was customary, when a person's body was to be hung on the cross or gibbet. (Deuteronomy xxi. 22; Josue x. 26; Lamentations v. 12; 1 Kings xxxi. 10.) --- *Birds.* So Horace says, *pasces in cruce corvos.*

VERSE 20

Birthday. This was a common practice among the pagans. (St. Matthew xiv. 6; 2 Machabees vi. 7.) (Calmet)

VERSE 23

Forgot. A thing too common among those who enjoy prosperity! (Haydock) --- God would not have his servants to trust in men. (Du Hamel) --- The butler was a figure of the good thief, as the baker represented the impenitent one, between whom our Savior hung on the cross. (Calmet)

CHAPTER XLI

VERSE 1

River; or the branch of the Nile which ran to Tanis, his capital. There were seven principal canals, and this was the most to the east, except that of Pelusium. (Calmet)

VERSE 2

Marshy. Hebrew *Achu;* a word which the Septuagint and Siracides (Ecclesiasticus xl. 16) retain. (Du Hamel)

VERSE 3

Very bank; to shOw that the Nile had not inundated far, and that consequently a great famine would prevail, as the fertility of Egypt depends greatly on the overflowing of the Nile. "When the river rises 12 cubits, sterility pervades Egypt; when 13, famine is still felt. Fourteen cubits bring joy, 15 security, 16 delight. It has never yet been known to rise above 18 cubits." (Pliny, Natural History v. 9.) This successive depression of the waters was an effect of God's judgments, which no astrologers could foretell. (Tirinus)

VERSE 5

Another dream of the same import, (ver. 25) to convince Pharao that the event would certainly take place, ver. 32. Thus Daniel had a double vision, Daniel vii. 2, 3. --- *One stalk.* It was of the species which Pliny (Natural History xviii. 10,) calls *ramosum,* branchy. What would strike Pharao the most was, that the last ears should devour the former ones. (Calmet)

VERSE 6

Blasted with the eastern wind, blowing from the deserts of Arabia, Osee xiii. 15. (Menochius)

VERSE 7

Rest. Hebrew adds, "and behold a dream" sent by God, like Solomon's, 3 Kings iii. 15. The king's mind was quite full of what he had seen.

VERSE 8

Interpreters: chartumim is probably an Egyptian word; denoting magicians, priests, and interpreters of their sacred books, hieroglyphics, &c. K. Ptolemy consulted them. (Tacitus, Hist. iv.)

VERSE 9

My sin against your majesty, and my ingratitude towards Joseph. (Calmet)

VERSE 12

Servant. Chap. xxxix. 4. He waited also upon the prisoners of rank, chap. xl. 4. (Haydock)

VERSE 14

Shaved him. The Egyptians let their hair grow, and neglected their persons, when they were in mourning or prison. But on other occasions they cut their hair in their youth. (Herod. ii. 36. iii. 12.) It was not lawful to appear in court in mourning attire. (Esther iv. 2; Genesis l. 4.) (Calmet)

VERSE 16

Without, &c. The interpretation does not proceed from any natural acquirement, but from God alone. (Chaldean) (Tirinus) --- The Samaritan and Aquila read, "Without me God will not give," &c. See Matthew x. 20.

VERSE 30

The land of Egypt, and the adjacent countries.

VERSE 34

Fifth part. This was a tax laid upon all the Egyptians, (Calmet) unless Pharao paid for what corn was laid up. (Haydock) --- This quantity would be sufficient, as the people would be content with a smaller allowance during the famine; and the environs of the Nile would produce something, though not worth mentioning, chap. xlv. 6. (Menochius)

VERSE 38

God. Hebrew, of the gods Elohim. Pharao was probably an idolater.

VERSE 40

Obey. Hebrew *Yishak;* which may signify also "kiss" you, or their hand, in testimony of respect; or "shall be fed, governed, and led forth," &c. *He made him master of his house, and ruler,* &c. (Psalm civ. 21; Wisdom x. 14.)

VERSE 42

His ring, the sign of power. Thus Alexander appointed Perdiccas to be his successor. (Curtius x. 5) Assuerus gave his authority to Aman and to Mardocheus, Esther iii. and viii. --- *Silk,* or fine cotton; *shes h*(or ssoss). See byssus, Exodus xxv. 4. --- *Chain,* with which the president of the senate in Egypt, or the chief justice, was adorned. The three chief officers among the Chaldees wore chains, Daniel v. 7, 16. (Calmet)

VERSE 43

Second chariot. On public occasions the king was followed by an empty chariot, (2 Paralipomenon xxxv. 24) or the chariot here spoken of, was destined for the person who was next in dignity to the king. (Calmet) --- *That all,* &c. Hebrew, "crying *Abroc,*" which Aquila explains in the same sense as the Vulgate. Others think it is an exclamation of joy, (Grotius) like huzza! (Haydock) or it may mean father of the king, *or* tender father, chap. xlv. 8.

VERSE 44

Pharao, or the king. This is the preamble to the decree for the exaltation of Joseph, which subjected to him the armies and all the people of Egypt.

VERSE 45

The savior of the world. Tsaphenath pahneach. (Challoner) --- In the Coptic language, which is derived from the Egyptian, *Psotemphane* is said to mean the savior of the world. St. Jerome supposed this word was not Hebrew; and therefore he added, *in the Egyptian tongue,* though he knew it might be interpreted in Hebrew "a revealer of secrets." (q. Heb.) --- *Putiphare.* Whether this person be the same with his old master, cannot easily be decided. Most people think he was not. See St. Chrysostom, 63. hom. --- *Priest.* None were esteemed more noble in Egypt. --- *Heliopolis.* Hebrew *On,* "the city of the sun," built on the banks of the Nile, about half a day's journey to the north of Memphis.

VERSE 47

Sheaves. The straw would serve to feed the cattle, and would hinder the corn from spoiling for 50 years, if kept from the air. (Varro; Pliny, Natural History xviii. 30.) (Calmet)

VERSE 51

Manasses. That is, *oblivion,* or *forgetting.* (Challoner) --- *Father's house,* or the injuries received from my brethren. (Haydock)

VERSE 52

Ephraim. That is, *fruitful,* or *growing.* (Challoner) --- Being in the plural number, it means "productions." ---*Poverty;* where I have been poor and afflicted, though now advanced in honor. (Haydock)

VERSE 55

World. Round about Egypt; such as Chanaan, Syria, &c. (Menochius) --- *There was.* The Syriac and some Latin copies, read *not,* &c.: there was a famine. We must adhere to the Vulgate and Hebrew.

VERSE 57

All provinces in the neighborhood for the stores laid up would not have supplied all mankind even for a few months. (Calmet)

CHAPTER XLII
VERSE 1

Careless. Hebrew, "gazing at one another," like idle people.

VERSE 6

To him. Conformably to the prophetic dreams, chap. xxxvii. 7, 9. (Menochius) --- Joseph was like a prince or sultan, *shallit,* with sovereign authority. (Calmet)

VERSE 8

By them. Years and change of situation had made such an alteration in him. God was pleased that Jacob should remain so long ignorant of his son's fate, that, by sorrow, he might do penance, and purify himself from every stain; and that he might not attempt to redeem Joseph, whose slavery was to be the source of so much good to his family. (Menochius) --- Joseph did not make himself known at first; in order to bring his brethren to a true sense of their duty, that they might obtain pardon for their sin. Thus pastors must sometimes treat their penitents with a degree of severity. (St. Gregory, hom. 22, Ezec.; St. Augustine, ser. 82, de Tem.) (Worthington)

VERSE 9

You are spies. This he said by way of examining them, to see what they would answer. (Challoner) --- Aquila translates "vagrants" going from place to place, as if to discover the weakest parts. Joseph was a person in authority. It was his duty to guard against invasion. He knew how his brethren had treated Sichem, and how they had behaved to himself; and though he might not suppose, that they had any evil design upon Egypt, yet he had a right to make them give an account of themselves. (Haydock) --- He wished also to extort from them a true account respecting Jacob and Benjamin. (Menochius)

VERSE 15

Health. This oath implies, that he is willing that even Pharao, whom he so much revered, should perish, if he did not execute what he said: (Haydock) or, as Pharao is now in health, so true it is you should not *all* depart, till your youngest brother come. (Calmet)

VERSE 16

Or else by the health of Pharao you are spies. That is, if these things you say be proved false, you are *to be held for spies* for your lying, and shall be treated as such. Joseph dealt in this manner with his brethren, to bring them by means of affliction to a sense of their former sin, and a sincere repentance for it.

VERSE 18

God. I shall do nothing contrary to justice or good faith, as I know I have a superior in heaven, to whom I must give an account. (Menochius)

VERSE 21

We deserve. Conscience upbraids. "Punishment opens the mouth, which sin had shut," St. Gregory. (Menochius) --- They had sold Joseph about 22 years before! (Calmet)

VERSE 22

His blood. Ruben supposed his brother was dead, (ver. 13) and judging that Jacob would not let Benjamin come, he thought they must all perish. (Haydock)

VERSE 23

Interpreter, to keep them at a greater distance. It does not appear that the sons of Jacob were ignorant of the language of the country. (Calmet)

VERSE 25

Simeon. If he had joined himself to Ruben and Juda, who seemed inclined to protect Joseph, they might easily have prevented the cruel act, by overawing their younger brothers. Hence he was most guilty. (Menochius) --- *Presence.* That they might learn to condole with an afflicted brother.

VERSE 34

And you may, &c. Joseph had said, (ver. 20) *and you may not die,* which they thus interpret. (Haydock)

VERSE 35

Astonished. One had before made the discovery, ver. 28. Now all find their *purses* among the corn, which renews their astonishment. (Calmet)

VERSE 36

Without. Through excess of grief, Jacob speaks with a degree of exaggeration; or he thought his children were now taken from him so fast, that he would soon have none left.

VERSE 37

Kill, &c. By this proposal, he meant to signify his utmost care and zeal to bring back young Benjamin safe to his father.

VERSE 38

Alone: the son of my beloved Rachel. (Haydock) --- *To hell.* That is, to that place where the souls then remained, as above, chap. xxxvii. ver. 35, (Challoner) though with respect to his *grey hairs,* and body, it may signify the grave. (Haydock)

CHAPTER XLIII

VERSE 5

My face, in peace. Joseph had told them they should be considered as spies, if they did not produce their youngest brother. (Menochius)

VERSE 7

Asked us. This is perfectly consonant with what they say, chap. xlii. 13 and chap. xliv. 19. They mentioned their having a brother at home, without the smallest suspicion of doing wrong.

VERSE 8

The boy; now 24 years old, (Calmet) and the father of a family, chap. xlvi. 21. (Haydock)

VERSE 9

Forever. Always lay the blame on me, and punish me as you think fit. (Menochius)

VERSE 11

Best fruits: Hebrew literally, "of the praise, *or* song of the earth;" or of those things for which the country is most renowned, and which are not found in Egypt. (Origen) --- *Balm.* Literally, *rosin, resinæ;* but here by that name is meant *balm.* (Challoner) See chap. xxxvii. 25. --- *Honey,* or all sorts of sweet fruit. --- *Storax:* Septuagint, "incense," or perfumes. It is like balm; thick, odoriferous, and medicinal. --- *Myrrh,* (stactes); Hebrew *Lot.* A liquor stamped from fresh myrrh pilled, with a little water. (Calmet) --- Sometimes it is translated *Gutta,* a drop. (Psalm xliv. 9.) (Menochius) --- *Turpentine.* St. Jerome and the Septuagint seem to have read *Bothmin* instead of the present Hebrew *Batenim,* which some translate, "nuts of the pistacium," (Bochart); which hand in clusters, and are of an oblong shape. Vitellius first brought them out of Syria. (Pliny, Natural History xv 22) --- *Almonds;* Septuagint *nuts,* of which almonds are one species. (Menochius)

VERSE 14

Desolate. Hebrew and Septuagint, "Since I am deprived of my children, I am deprived of my children:" I must submit.

VERSE 16

Victims: the blood of which was first offered to God, as he had appointed, (chap. xviii. 1; Leviticus xvii. 5) and the flesh brought upon the table. If idolatry was then common in Egypt, as Calmet supposes, in opposition to Grotius, Joseph did not participate at least in that impiety. --- *At noon.* This was the time for the chief meal in Egypt. The Hebrews generally took something at this time, and again in the evening. To eat before noon was esteemed a mark of intemperance. (Ecclesiastes x. 16; Acts ii. 15.) Plato thought the people of Italy, who eat two full meals in the day, would never be eminent for wisdom or for prudence. (Atheneus iv. 10.) (Calmet)

VERSE 21

We opened. Chap. xlii. 35. They seem to have discovered the whole of their money only when they were in the presence of Jacob; though they had already, perhaps, seen part of it at the inn, and left it in their sacks for the satisfaction of their father. (Haydock)

VERSE 23

Your God. To Him we must always refer what advantage we derive from men. He inspired Joseph to give such orders to his steward. --- *I have for good.* I received it, and was satisfied that it was good: you need not be uneasy; you are not suspected of any fraud. (Haydock) --- Hebrew, "Your money came into my hands." (Menochius)

VERSE 28

Living. The Samaritan and Septuagint add, "Joseph replied, Blessed be he of God: and bowing themselves," &c. Thus all Joseph's brethren adore him, chap. xxxvii. 7. (Haydock)

VERSE 32

Hebrews. "They had the same aversion for all who did not adopt their superstition." (Porphyrius, Abstin. iv.) Herod. ii. 41, says, that would not use a knife which had been in the hands of a Greek, nor kiss him. This aversion arose, from their custom of abstaining from various meats which other nations eat. (Chaldean; &c.) They disliked the Hebrews, because they were also *shepherds,* chap. xlvi. 34 (Calmet); and because they knew they were accustomed to eat goats, oxen, and sheep, the objects of adoration in Egypt, (Exodus viii. 26) though they were not, probably, served upon Joseph's table. (Tirinus) --- They who dwelt in the towns could not bear even the Egyptian shepherds, because they were of a more stirring and warlike temper. (Calmet) (Cunæus)

VERSE 36

They sat. This posture is more ancient than that of lying down at table. The Hebrews adopted the latter, from the Persians, during the captivity, Esther i. 6, and vii. 8. --- We have at least no earlier vestige of this custom in Scripture. (Calmet) --- *Very much* as they were placed in that order by the steward. They knew not how he could so exactly discover who was born first, as there was so short an interval between the births of many of them. (Haydock)

VERSE 34

Of him. Joseph, the master of the feast, sends a portion to each of his guests, according to the ancient custom. (Plut.[Plutarch] Sympos. ii.) --- *Five parts:* in order to distinguish Benjamin the more. So Hector reproaches Diomed for fleeing before him, though he was placed in the highest place at table among the Greeks, and had the largest portion both of meat and drink. --- *Merry. Inebriati sunt,* sometimes means intoxicated: but it is not at all probably that Joseph's brethren would indulge in any such excess, while they knew him not, (Calmet) and were under the impressions of fear and wonder. They took what was sufficient, and even decently abundant, with thankfulness for so unexpected an honor. (Haydock) --- The word is often taken in this sense, as at the feast of Cana, where Jesus would never have furnished such an abundance of wine for people already drunk. (John ii. 10; Proverbs xi. 24.) Homer's feasts consist in every man taking what he pleased. (Calmet)

CHAPTER XLIV

VERSE 4

Pursue; escorted by a troop of horsemen, to prevent resistance. (Menochius)

VERSE 5

To divine. This was spoken by Joseph to his steward in jest; alluding to the notion of the people, who took him to be a diviner. (Challoner) --- St. Thomas Aquinas, [Summa Theologiae] 2, 2, q. 195, a. 7. Hebrew may be translated without attending to the points, "Is not this the cup, out of which my lord drinketh; and he has augured, *or* discovered, by it the evil which you have committed." Pliny (Natural History xxx. 2) mentions a method of divining, by means of water in a basin. (Calmet) --- The Egyptians probably supposed that Joseph used some means to disclose what was hidden; and he alludes, in jest, to their foolish notion. (Haydock) --- He had a right to afflict his guilty brethren; and as for Benjamin, who was innocent, he made him ample recompense for this transitory terror. Some think that the steward said, *in which he is wont to divine,* unauthorized by his master. (Menochius)

VERSE 10

Sentence. It is but just; yet I shall only insist on the detention of the culprit. (Calmet) --- Joseph wished to see whether the marks of attention, which he had shown to Benjamin, would have excited the envy of his brethren (Menochius); and whether they would be concerned for him: thus he would discover their present dispositions. He might wish also to keep his younger brother out of danger, in case they were inclined to persecute him. (Haydock)

VERSE 13

The town, with heavy hearts, of which their torn garments were signs (Haydock): yet they say not a word in condemnation of Benjamin. They are determined either to clear him, or never to return home. (Menochius)

VERSE 14

Juda, mindful of his engagement, (chap. xliii. 9) and perhaps more eloquent and bolder than the rest. (Menochius)

VERSE 15

The science of divining. He speaks of himself according to what he was esteemed in that kingdom. And, indeed, he being truly a prophet, knew more without comparison than any of the Egyptian sorcerers. (Challoner) --- Hebrew, Septuagint, and Chaldean, "knew ye not that a man like me would divine with certainty," and presently discover any fraud? (Calmet)

VERSE 16

Iniquity. He begins with the greatest humility, acknowledging that they were justly punished by God for some transgression, though they were, in his opinion, innocent of any theft. (Haydock) --- Perhaps he might imagine that Benjamin had been guilty, (Bonfrere) and is willing to bear a part of the blame with the rest; or his conscience still presents before him the injustice done to Joseph so long before. (Haydock)

VERSE 18

Boldly, perceiving that he had to deal with an equitable judge. --- *Thou art;* the second man in the kingdom. Hebrew, "even as Pharao."

VERSE 20

Is left of, (habet mater.) Rachel had been dead about twenty-four years. (Haydock)

VERSE 31

With us, is not now found in Hebrew. But it is in the Samaritan, Septuagint, Syriac and Chaldean. (Calmet) --- *His grey hairs.* That is, his person, now far advanced in years. --- *With sorrow unto hell.* The Hebrew word for *hell* is here *Sheola,* the Greek *hades:* it is not taken for the *hell* of the damned; but for that place of souls below, where the servants of God were kept before the coming of Christ. Which place, both in the Scripture and in the creed, is named *hell.* (Challoner) --- In this speech, we find many particulars not mentioned before; whence it appears, that the sacred historian does not always specify every circumstance. But, in relating the same speech, uses various expressions to the same purport. (Calmet)

VERSE 33

The boy. I am older, and more fit for service. (Menochius)

VERSE 34

My father; who will drop down dead, oppressed with grief. How eloquent and pathetic was this address! Joseph could bear no more.

CHAPTER XLV
VERSE 2

Weeping, with a loud cry, being unable to restrain himself. The servants, who were in the adjoining apartments, heard this cry and declaration of Joseph, acknowledging one common father with these men; and they presently conveyed the intelligence to the king. (Haydock)

VERSE 4

Nearer; that no one might hear what he was going to say respecting their fault. (Menochius) --- It is thus we ought to treat those who have injured us. He excuses his brethren as much as possible. (Haydock)

VERSE 5

Hard. Hebrew, "Be not indignant in your eyes." Perhaps he was afraid, lest they should begin to accuse one another, as the authors of the deed, and thus disturb the harmony of this reconciliation. He perfectly understands the conduct of divine Providence, which can draw good out of evil, and cause even the malice of men to co-operate in the execution of his designs. (Calmet) --- God did not sanction or *will* this malice, as Calvin, &c., impiously assert. (Tirinus)

VERSE 6

Reaping, as in common years, thought he places near the Nile might produce some little; (Menochius) and hence the Egyptians ask Joseph for seed, chap. xlvii. 19. (Calmet)

VERSE 8

Counsel. Joseph's brethren had no design of elevating him to so high a dignity; but God's *will* directed Pharao to appoint him his counselor or prime minister. His *father.* (Haydock) --- So the Roman emperors styled the prefects of the Prætorium, and the Caliphs their chief minister. (Calmet)

VERSE 10

Gessen, to the northeast of Egypt, *near me,* at Tanis, in the Delta and near the promised land, being a part of Arabia. (Haydock) --- Heliopolis, where many suppose Joseph resided, is situated in the same canton, and was one of the chief cities after Ramesse, the capital, chap. xlvi. 28. This country is often refreshed by showers of rain, (Calmet) which never falls in most parts of Egypt. It is intersected by many canals, and is very rich and proper for pasturage. (Haydock)

VERSE 11

Perish. Hebrew, be reduced to poverty. He fed them like the priests, chap. xlvii. 12, 22. (Calmet)

VERSE 12

My mouth. You now recognize my features and my speech; particularly you, my dear Benjamin. (Haydock) --- I speak no longer by an interpreter. (Menochius)

VERSE 16

Family, and courtiers. They were all so enraptured with Joseph's conduct, that they rejoiced in whatever gave him pleasure. (Menochius) --- They thought, perhaps, that his relations would resemble him, and be of service to Egypt. (Haydock)

VERSE 18

Marrow; which is an emphatical expression, to signify the *best things of Egypt,* Chaldean. Hebrew, "the fat, *or* the cream of the land." (Calmet)

VERSE 20

Leave nothing. Hebrew may have another meaning, which Calmet approves, "Let not your eye spare your furniture." Be not concerned to leave what may be useless, as most of the husbandry utensils would be in Egypt, "for all," &c.

Two robes (*stolas*) hanging down to the feet. These properly belong to women. But they are worn by men in the East. It was customary to make presents of such robes, as it is still among the great men and kings of that country. Lucullus kept 6000 cloaks in his wardrobe. (Horat. 1. sat. 2.) (Calmet) --- *Of silver,* sicles. The Septuagint has "of gold," as also chap. xxxvii. 28.

VERSE 23

As much...besides. This is omitted in Hebrew or at least is left ambiguous, "He sent in like manner to his father ten," &c. But the Syriac and Septuagint explain it like the Vulgate. --- *She-asses.* Septuagint, "mules." --- *Bread.* Hebrew adds, "meat," *or* provisions. (Calmet) --- These presents might convince Jacob that Joseph was still alive. (Haydock)

VERSE 24

Angry. A prudent admonition at all times, but particularly now, to Joseph's brethren; lest reflecting on his excessive kindness, they should each wish to remove from themselves the stigma of cruelty towards him, by throwing it upon others. (Haydock) --- Hebrew may be rendered, "fear not." (Calmet)

VERSE 26

He awaked, &c. His heart was overpowered between hope and distrust. He seemed to himself to be dreaming. Septuagint, "in an ecstasy." Such a sudden transition has oftentimes caused death. (Haydock)

VERSE 27

Revived; like a lamp, which was just going out, for want of oil, resumes fresh vigor when a new supply is poured in. (St. Chrysostom)

CHAPTER XLVI
VERSE 1

The well of the oath. Bersabee.

VERSE 3

Fear not. He might be apprehensive, lest his children should be depraved, living among idolaters, or prefer Egypt before the promised land. He was also afraid to undertake this journey without consulting God. (Menochius)

VERSE 4

Thence; in thy posterity. Septuagint add *at last,* or after a long time. Jacob's bones were brought back and buried in Chanaan. (Calmet) --- *Eyes,* as he is the most dear to thee. Parents closed the eyes of their children in death. The Romans opened them again when the corpse was upon the funeral pire; thinking it a mark of disrespect for the eyes to be shut to heaven; "ut neque ab homine supremum eos spectari fas sit, *& cælo non ostendi, nefas.*" (Pliny, xi. 37.)

VERSE 7

Daughters. Dina, and grand-daughter Sara, (ver. 17) and his sons' wives, &c. (Calmet) --- We may observe, that all here mentioned were not born at the time when Jacob went down into Egypt, but they were before he or Joseph died; that is, during the space of 17 or 71 years. See St. Augustine, q. 151, 173. (Menochius) --- The names of the Hebrew and Septuagint vary some little from the Vulgate, which may be attributed to the difference of pronunciation, or to the same person having many names. The number is also different in the Septuagint as the authors of that version have, perhaps, inserted some names taken from other parts of Scripture, to remove any apparent contradiction. The genealogies of Juda, Joseph, and Benjamin, are carried farther than the rest, as those families were of greater consequence.

VERSE 9

Hesron and *Charmi* were probably born in Egypt, as Ruben had only two sons, chap. xlii. 37. (Philo.)

VERSE 10

Jamuel. Numbers xxvi. 12, he is called Namuel. --- *Jachin* is *Jarid,* 1 Paralipomenon iv. 24. (Calmet)

VERSE 12

Were born, afterwards. (Menochius)

VERSE 15

Syria. This must be restrained to her seven children. --- *Thirty-three,* comprising Lia, or Jacob; but without Her and Onan, who were dead. (Calmet)

VERSE 20

Ephraim. The Septuagint take in here the children of both, Numbers xxvi. 29, 35.

VERSE 21

Benjamin. Ten in number; though the Septuagint have only nine, and suppose that some of them were his grandchildren. He was 33 (or 24, Menochius) years old. (Calmet) --- Grotius thinks three names have been made out of two; *Echi, Ros,* and *mophim,* out of *Ahiram* and *Supham,* as we read, Numbers xxvi. 38.

VERSE 23

Sons. The Arabic has *son. Husim* is Suham, (Numbers xxvi. 42) by change and transposition of letters. (Kennicott)

VERSE 26

Sixty-six; not including Jacob, Joseph, and his two children, who make up 70, ver. 27. (Deuteronomy x. 22.) The Septuagint taking in Joseph's grandchildren, read 75; in which they are followed by St. Stephen, Acts. vii. 14. See St. Jerome q. Heb. (Calmet) --- St. Augustine cannot account for these grand-children and great grand-children of Joseph being mentioned as coming with Jacob into Egypt, since some of them were not born during his life-time. He suspects some hidden mystery. (Worthington) See ver. 7. --- Some think St. Stephen excludes Jacob, Joseph, and his sons; and included the 64 men, with 11 wives. (Du Hamel)

VERSE 34

Abomination. See chap. xliii. 32. The source of this hatred against foreign shepherds, was probably because, about 100 years before Abraham, the shepherd-kings, *Hycussos,* had got possession of a great part of Egypt, and were at last expelled by the kings of Thebais. See Manetho ap. Eusebius, Præp. x. 13. Another reason why they hated foreigners was, because they slew and eat sheep, &c., which they themselves adored. The Egyptians kept sheep for this purpose, and for the benefits to be derived from their wool, &c., chap. xlvii. 17. (Calmet) --- Joseph took advantage of this disposition of the inhabitants, to keep his brethren at a distance from them, that they might not be perverted. He does not introduce them at court, that no jealousy might be excited. He shows that he is not ashamed of his extraction. (Menochius)

CHAPTER XLVII

VERSE 2

The last. Extremos. Some interpret this word of the *chiefest,* and *most slightly* but Joseph seems rather to have chosen out such as had the meanest appearance, that Pharao might not think of employing them at court, with danger of their morals and religion; (Challoner) or in the army, where they might be distracted with many cares, and be too much separated from one another. (Haydock) --- He took such of his brethren as came first at hand. (Vatable)

VERSE 7

Blessed him, Pharao; saying, perhaps, *God save the king;* or, *O king live forever:* thus wishing that he might enjoy all sorts of blessings. (Menochius) --- It is generally taken in this sense, when men bless one another; but when they bless God, they mean to praise, supplicate, or thank him. (Calmet)

VERSE 9

Pilgrimage. He hardly deigns to style it *life,* as he was worn out with labor and sorrows, and was drawing fast to an end, so much sooner than his ancestors. Isaac had lived 180 years, and was only dead the year before Joseph was made ruler of Egypt. Some had lived above 900 years. (Haydock)

VERSE 13

Chanaan. The whole world that was inhabited, and known to the Hebrews, felt perhaps the effect of this raging famine; but the countries here mentioned were the most afflicted. (Haydock)

VERSE 14

Treasure, reserving nothing for himself. (Philo)

VERSE 15

Wanted. Or "failed both in Egypt and Chanaan," as the Hebrew insinuates. (Haydock)

VERSE 18

Second; or the next *year* after they had sold their cattle; the fourth of the famine, or perhaps the last, since they ask for seed, ver. 19. In that year, Joseph gave back the cattle, &c., to the Egyptians, on condition that they should ever after pay the fifth part of the products of the land to the king, the sole proprietor, who had thus full authority to send them to till any part of his dominions. (Calmet)

VERSE 19

Servants. A person may part with his liberty, to preserve life. (Menochius)

VERSE 21

People, "he transplanted" *from,* &c., as the Hebrew, Arabic, &c., now read, by the change of one letter. Herodotus, ii. 108, says, the same person has never a field there two years together. Didorus 1, also attests, that individuals have no property in Egypt, the land being divided among the priests, the king, and the military. Tradesmen always follow their father's profession, which makes them very skilful.

VERSE 22

Priests. This was done by the king's direction, as they were probably idolaters. (Menochius) --- The immunities of the sacred ministers have been respected both by Pagans, Jews, and Christians; by all who have had any sentiments of religion. Reason dictates that they should live by the altar. They have to labor for the truest interests of the people, and consequently are worthy of their hire. --- *Which had been given,* &c. Inasmuch as their wants were supplied, and the king forebore to claim their land. Hebrew, "only the land of the priests he, *Joseph,* bought not." (Haydock) --- If infidels did so much for their priests, ought we to do less for those of God? (St. Chrysostom, hom. 65.) (Worthington)

VERSE 26

This day. When Moses wrote, and long after, as we learn from Josephus, Clement of Alexandria, Diodorus, &c. (Calmet)

VERSE 29

Thigh. To swear, as the steward of Abraham did, chap. xxiv. 2. --- *Kindness and truth.* This act of real mercy; or, show me *mercy,* by promising freely to comply with my request; and *truth,* by fulfilling this oath. (Menochius)

VERSE 30

Place. Hebron, where Sara, Abraham, and Isaac reposed. (Calmet) --- Thus he manifested his belief in a future resurrection with his Savior, who should be born in that land; and he admonished his descendants never to lose sight of it, nor forfeit the promises by their wicked conduct, chap. xxiii. 17. (Menochius) --- He teaches us likewise, to be solicitous to obtain Christian burial. (Worthington)

VERSE 31

To the bed's head. St. Paul, (Hebrews xi. 21) following the Greek translation of the Septuagint, reads *adored the top of his rod.* Where note that the same word in the Hebrew, according to the different pointing of it, signifies both a *bed* and a *rod.* And to verify both these sentences, we must understand that Jacob, leaning on Joseph's rod, adored, turning towards the head of his bed which adoration, inasmuch as it was referred to God, was an absolute, and sovereign worship but inasmuch as it was referred to the rod of Joseph, as a figure of the scepter, that is, of the royal dignity of Christ, was only an inferior and relative honor. (Challoner) --- St. Augustine proposes another very probable explanation. He adored God, supporting himself on the top of his staff, or of Joseph's scepter, q. 162. The Septuagint and Syriac intimate, that Jacob bowed down respectfully towards the scepter of his son, and thus complied with the explication which he had given to his dream, chap. xxxvii. 10. Others, who understand the Hebrew *Hamitta,* in the sense given to it by St. Jerome, Aquila, and Symmachus, suppose that after he had given his last instructions to Joseph in a sitting posture, growing weaker, he laid his head again upon his pillow. (Calmet) ---God was pleased to have this recorded in a language subject to such various interpretations; as he, perhaps, would have us to understand, that Jacob literally bowed down both to the bed-head and to the top of the scepter. For many believe that the Scripture has often several literal meanings. (Tirinus) --- If the Massoretic points had been known to the Septuagint, we should not have had this variation. But the learned generally agree, that they are of human, and even of very modern invention.

CHAPTER XLVIII

VERSE 1

Sick. Worse than when he was with him before. (Haydock)

VERSE 2

Strengthened: with the thought of seeing this beloved son, and also with the prophetic spirit (Menochius) of God, which filled him with joy, &c, Galatians v. 22. (Haydock)

VERSE 4

Possession. He makes mention of this first vision of God to him, to show that he had a right to Chanaan, and to adopt the two children of Joseph, who were each to have as much as his own children. (Haydock) --- Jacob's posterity enjoyed that land till the Messiah came, with some few interruptions. But his spiritual children inherit a much better country, (of which this was a figure) an eternal kingdom in heaven. (Calmet)

VERSE 5

Mine, by adoption; and shall be heads of their respective tribes. (Menochius)

VERSE 6

Thine. They shall not claim the same prerogative: they shall live among their brethren, Ephraim and Manasses. We read not that Joseph had any other children besides these two. (Calmet) --- The double portion, or the birth-right, was thus transferred from Ruben to Joseph. (Du Hamel)

VERSE 7

For when, &c. Hebrew, "as for me." Do not wonder that I should so earnestly desire to be laid in the tomb of Mambre, whereas your mother was buried at Ephrata. I was in a manner forced to bury her there, by the heat of the weather, (Menochius) and the confusion to which my family was then exposed, on account of the slaughter of the Sichemites. (Haydock) --- That place was, moreover, to be honored with the birth of the Messias. (St. Augustine, q. 165.)

VERSE 11

Deprived. Hebrew, "I did not *expect;* or, I durst not *pray*" to God for a thing which I thought impossible; I mean, the happiness of *seeing thee;* and lo, God, &c.

VERSE 12

Lap, (*gremio, breast,*) after Jacob had embraced them; or from between his knees, where they knelt to receive his blessing. --- *Bowed down,* out of reverence to his father, and to beg of God that he would put words of comfort into the mouth of his father, on this solemn and important occasion. Then, in order that his children might not lean upon, or incommode Jacob, he placed them, the elder at his right-hand, the other at his left. (Haydock)

VERSE 14

Changing. Hebrew, "making his hands intelligent;" or giving to understand, by forming a cross with his extended hands, that he had some particular reason for so doing. (Haydock) --- By the preference given to Ephraim, he forshowed his royal dignity, in giving kings to the ten tribes, (Eusebius) and that his tribe would surpass that of his brother in glory and numbers; (ver. 19) and lastly, give birth to that great leader, Josue; who, as a figure of Christ, should introduce the Israelites into the promised land. (Menochius) --- The custom of imposing hands on a person, is of high antiquity, and is still practiced in the Christian church in the ordination of her ministers. (Numbers viii. 10; Acts vi. 6.) See Matthew xix. 13; Numbers xxvii. 23. (Calmet) --- The cross of Christ is the source of all our exaltation. A preference for the younger children is generally observable in Scripture; being intended to show that the Church, though chosen later out of all nations, should obtain the preference over the synagogue. (Theodoret) (Tirinus)

VERSE 16

The angel guardian, who, by God's ordinance, has ever protected me, continue his kind attention towards these my grand-children. It is not probably that he, who was called God before, should now be styled an angel, as some Protestants would have us believe. (Haydock) --- St. Basil (contra Eunom. iii.) and St. Chrysostom, with many others, allege this text, to prove that an angel is given to man for the direction of his life, and to protect him against the assaults of the rebel angels, as Calvin himself dares not deny. ---*Let my,* &c. Let them partake of the blessings (promised by name to me, to Abraham, and to Isaac) among the other tribes; or, may God bless them, in consideration of his servants. Moses obtained pardon for the Hebrews, by reminding God of these his chosen friends, Exodus xxxii. (Worthington)

VERSE 17

Displeased; (graviter accepit) was grieved to see the elder son neglected; and, thinking it might possibly proceed from a mistake, as his father's eyes were so dim that he did not know them, (ver. 8) he ventured to suggest his sentiments to his father; but acquiesced in his decision. (Haydock) --- The greatest prophets are not always under actual inspiration. (Calmet)

VERSE 19

A people, (in populos). He shall be father of many peoples. The tribe of Manasses was divided, and had a large territory on either side of the Jordan, immediately north of that which fell to the lots of Ephraim and of Gad. (Haydock) --- *Grow.* Hebrew, "shall be the fullness of nations;" or shall possess everything that can make a nation great and enviable. The event justified this prediction. Ephraim was at the head of the ten tribes, most valiant and powerful, 3 Kings xi. 26. (Calmet)

VERSE 20

In thee, Joseph. Septuagint, "in you," Ephraim and Manasses. The Israelites shall wish the same happiness to their greatest friends, as that which you have enjoyed. (Menochius)

VERSE 22

Thee. In thy posterity; and particularly in Ephraim, to whose lot it shall fall, *a portion.* Hebrew *shecem;* which the Septuagint explain of the city, or field near it, which Jacob had formerly purchased; and which, being wrested from him after he had left that country, by the Amorrhites, he recovered by the sword. (Masius.) --- The particulars of this transaction are not given in Scripture. (Menochius) --- The children of Joseph buried their father in this field, Josue xxiv. 32. There also was Jacob's well, John iv. 5. We have already observed, that Jacob restored whatever his sons had taken unjustly from the unhappy Sichemites, chap. xxxiv. 30. --- *Sword and bow,* is understood by St. Jerome and Onkelos in a spiritual sense, to denote his justice and earnest prayer, by which he merited the divine protection; (Calmet) or it may mean the money, which he had procured with hard labor.

CHAPTER XLIX

VERSE 1

Last. Hebrew, "future days." It was an ancient and commendable custom, for parents to assemble their children in their last moments, to give them salutary instructions. They often also foretold to them what should happen. See Deuteronomy xxxi; Josue xxiv; 1 Kings xii; Tobias iv. 3; 1 Machabees ii. Cyrus and Socrates both believed that they had then an insight into futurity. (Calmet)

VERSE 3

My strength, &c. He calls him his *strength,* as being born whilst his father was in his full strength and vigor; he calls him *the beginning of his sorrow,* because *cares* and *sorrows* usually come on with the birth of children. ---*Excelling in gifts,* &c., because the first-born had a title to a *double portion ,* and to have the command over his brethren, which Ruben forfeited by his sin; being *poured out as water;* that is, spilt and lost. (Challoner) --- *In command.* He ought to have succeeded to his father in authority. But Joseph entered in upon his rejection, 1 Paralipomenon v. 1. The priesthood was given to Levi's descendants; and the regal power, partly to those of Joseph, who reigned over the ten tribes, for a long time; and partly to the posterity of Juda, who exercised dominion over all the people of Israel. (Chaldee) (Worthington)

VERSE 4

Grow thou not. This was not meant by way of a curse or imprecation; but by way of a prophecy, foretelling that the tribe of Ruben should not inherit the pre-eminences usually annexed to the first birth-right, viz., the double portion, the being prince or lord over the other brethren, and the priesthood: of which the double portion was given to Joseph, the princely office to Juda, and the priesthood to Levi. (Challoner) --- Thou hast abandoned thyself to thy brutal passion; do so no more, *ne adjicias.* (St. Jerome, q. Heb.) *Let Ruben live, and die not; let him be small in number,* Deuteronomy xxxiii. 6. His tribe never became very considerable. (Calmet) --- *Couch.* See chap xxxv. 22. Eternal infamy attends the name of Ruben. (Haydock)

VERSE 5

Brethren. Born of the same parents; similar in disposition. --- *Vessels;* instruments. Septuagint and Chaldean, "they have completed wickedness," as they read *calu,* instead of the present Hebrew *cele,* which is adopted by Aquila. (Calmet)

VERSE 6

Slew a man, viz., Sichem, the son of Hemor, with all his people, chap. xxxiv. Mystically and prophetically it alludes to Christ; whom their posterity, viz., the priests and the scribes, put to death. (Challoner) --- *A wall,* Sichem, which they destroyed: or, according to the Septuagint, "they ham-strung" *a bull,* as the same Hebrew word signifies; both which may refer to the prince of the town, or to Joseph, (Calmet) in whose persecution these two were principally concerned. Jacob declares, he had no share in their attack upon the people of Sichem: his *soul,* or his *glory,* was not impaired by their misconduct. (Haydock)

VERSE 7

Scatter them. Levi had no division allotted to him, but only some cities among the other tribes; and Simeon had only a part of Juda's lot, which was so small, that his descendants were forced to seek for a fresh establishment; some in Gader, others in Mount Seir. (1 Paralipomenon iv. 39; Josue xix. 2.) Simeon alone was not blessed by Moses, Deuteronomy xxxiii. (Du Hamel) --- The Levites obtained a blessing, on account of their distinguished zeal; (Numbers xxv.) while Zambri rivets, as it were, the curse upon the family of Simeon. (Menochius)

VERSE 8

Praise. He alludes to his name, his martial prowess, and dominion over all his *brethren;* who should be all called Jews, and submit to his sway. Some explain all this of Jesus Christ; others refer the first part of the prophecy to Juda. (Haydock)

VERSE 9

A lion's whelp, &c. This blessing of Juda foretell the strength of his tribe, the fertility of his inheritance, and principally that the scepter, and legislative power, should not be utterly taken away from his race till about the time of the coming of Christ: as in effect it never was: which is a demonstration against the modern Jews, that the Messias is long since come; for the scepter has long since been utterly taken away from Juda. (Challoner) --- This none can deny. Juda is compared to *a lion,* which was the emblem of his royal dignity, and was borne in the standards of that tribe. --- *To the prey.* Hebrew, "from the prey." He proceeds from victory to victory. He *couches,* ready to fall upon his prey; and, retiring to the mountains, is still eager to renew the attack. (Calmet) --- Read the history of David and of Solomon, who, both in peace and war, were a terror to the surrounding nations.

VERSE 10

The scepter. Almost every word in this verse has been explained in a different manner. But all the ancient Jews agree with Christians, that it contains a prediction of the Messias, and points out the period of his coming. Whether this was verified when Herod, a foreigner, got possession of the throne, and was acknowledged by the Jews, just about the time of our Savior's nativity, as most of the fathers suppose; or it only took its full effect when Agrippa II lost all his power, the temple and the city were laid in ruins, and the whole nation dispersed forever, it is not perhaps so easy to determine. In either supposition, the Messias has long since come. Jacob foretells, either that Christ would make his appearance as soon as the Jews should fall under a foreign yoke, and in this sense he was born about the 37th year of Herod the great --- or he should come just before the kingdom of Juda should have an end, which took place in the 70th year of the Christian era, or about 37 years after the public appearance and death of our Savior. *The scepter shall not depart* irrevocably from the Jews; over whom the tribe of Juda had always the greatest authority in appointing the princes, when they were not selected from the tribe itself, or *from his thigh; till the Messias,* who has been expected so long, shall come and gather *all nations* into his Church. Then the designs of Providence, in watching over the Jews, being accomplished, their republic shall be dissolved, because they have shed his *blood,* instead of acknowledging his celestial beauty, ver. 12. The evident signs of decay in the kingdom of the Jews, were sufficient to excite the attention of all to look for the Messias; and we read, both in St. John iv. 25, in Tacitus, and Suetonius, that his appearance was fully expected about that time. The *scepter* is the emblem of sovereign, though not always independent, power. Juda and his posterity were always at the head of their brethren. They marched first in the wilderness; two of the judges were of this tribe. But their chief glory began with David, whose posterity the whole nation obeyed, till Jeroboam tore away the ten tribes. Still the tribe of Benjamin and the Levites adhered to Juda. During the captivity there were judges admitted to superintend over their brethren; and King Joakim was raised to high authority. The rulers who came into power after the return of the Jews, were either of this tribe, at least by the mother's side, or were chosen and recognized by the tribe of Juda. Even Herod, in this sense, might be considered as a Jewish king, though a foreigner, as well as a Thracian might be counted a Roman emperor, without any diminution of the imperial authority of Rome. Perhaps, indeed, he was an usurper, till the nation acknowledged his authority two years after the birth of Christ. (Philo, de Temp. ii; Josephus, Antiquities xvii. 3.) "Herod was the first foreign king admitted by the Jews." (St. Augustine, City of God xviii. 45.) If, therefore, no stranger was to be acknowledged by the nation, till He came, who was to establish a spiritual and everlasting kingdom, the moment was arrived, when the Jews submitted to Herod, and Christ had actually been born two years. --- *From Juda,* or from that tribe; for Jacob gave peculiar blessings to each; (ver. 28) and hence the fathers gather, that the Messias should spring from Juda. --- *Ruler from his thigh,* lineally descended from him, or acknowledged at least by his posterity, as all the legal princes were till the coming of Christ. --- *Mechokek* might also signify a teacher or scribe expounding the law of Moses, which subsisted for the same period; but this is more probably a farther explication of the *scepter,* &c. (Calmet) -- - *Till had ci,* which words being joined together, are always taken in this sense. (Helvicus.) --- *Sent. Schiloach* (or *Ssolue*) seems to have been in St. Jerome's copy, though we now read *Shiloh* (or *Ssole*) "to whom" the authority belongs; Septuagint, "to whom all things are reserved; *or* till the things arrive, which are laid up for him. (Calmet) ---*Expectation,* or congregation of *nations,* as Aggeus afterwards foretold, ii. 8. If we examine all the plausible explications which have been given to this verse, we shall find that they all tend to convey the same truth. "The scepter (ssebet, rod, crook, power or tribe) shall not depart (cease, be taken off) from Juda, (the tribe or the Jews) nor a leader (scribe, lawyer, or legislator) from his thigh, (between his feet, or from his banners) till He, who shall be sent, (shio, the pacific, his son, to whom it is, or the things are, reserved) arrive; and Him shall the nations expect, (and obey) to Him they shall look up (and be gathered). Whom will the Jews point out to whom all these characters agree, except our divine Lord, whom they also must one day adore? (Haydock)

VERSE 11

Foal. The nations, which had not been subjected to the yoke of the old law. --- *Vineyard;* the house of Israel, the *vineyard* of the Lord of hosts, Isaias v. 7. Christ broke down the wall of separation, and made *both one,* Ephesians ii. 14. --- *His ass,* or the Jews. --- *O my son;* Juda, the Savior king, who shall be born of thee, shall tie both Jews and Gentiles to the *vine,* which is himself, John xv. To the Jews he shall preach in person; but the Gentiles he shall call by his apostles, chosen out of the vineyard of the Jewish church. (Menochius) --- *He shall wash his robe,* his flesh, and *his garment,* or all his disciples, in his own *blood;* adorning them with all graces by means of his death, which must be applied to their souls, in the holy sacraments devoutly received, and in the Mass, where his blood is offered under the appearance of *wine.* (Haydock) See St. Ambrose, &c. Tertullian, (against Marc. iv) showing that Christ fulfilled the figures of the old law, interprets the stole to mean his body, and wine his blood. (Worthington) --- Jacob alludes also to fertility and abundance of vines, which should enrich the portion of Juda, particularly about Engaddi, Canticle of Canticles i. 13. (Calmet)

VERSE 12

Beautiful. The eyes and teeth contribute much to the beauty of a face. Our Savior, rising form the dead, filled the hearts foR the beholders with joy, as wine exhilarates the heart of man. (Menochius) --- The spouse in the Canticle of Canticles, (ver. 12) compares the eyes of the bridegroom to the shining reddish, or fiery ones of pigeons: *chaclili,* beautiful, means shining red, &c. Jesus Christ seems to allude to this prophecy of Jacob, (Matthew xxi. 43 and John x 16) telling the Jews, that the *kingdom of God* should be taken from them, and *one fold* should be established for all. God would then cease to distinguish the Jews by any other marks than those of his wrath. He would no longer be their king and shepherd. His scepter, or pastoral crook, should be taken off the tribe of Juda, and it should be confounded with the rest, as it is at this day. (Calmet)

VERSE 13

Road. The territory of Zabulon was famous for good harbors, being situated between the Mediterranean and the sea of Genezareth. (Menochius) --- Jacob marks out the limits to be assigned his children, 200 years before Chanaan was conquered; and Moses wrote this before they possessed a foot of land in it. The reason why Zabulon is placed before his elder brother Issachar, is not known. --- *Sidon;* not the city, but the territory of Sidon, or Phenicia. (Calmet)

VERSE 14

Strong. Hebrew, "bony ass." Many of Jacob's children are compared to animals, which was customary in the eastern style. Homer compares Ajax with the ass, for his strength and patience, Iliad xii. Jacob thus indicates the laborious disposition of Issachar's tribe, which did not delight in war. Their country was the most fruitful of all Galilee. (Calmet)

VERSE 16

Dan shall judge, &c. This was verified in Samson, who was of the tribe of Dan, and began to deliver Israel, Judges xiii. 5. But as this deliverance was but temporal and very imperfect, the holy patriarch (ver. 18) aspires after another kind of deliverer, saying: *I will look for thy salvation, O Lord.* (Challoner) --- Many have supposed that Antichrist will be one of his descendants, which makes Jacob break out into this exclamation. (Haydock) --- See St. Irenæus, Against Heresies v. 30, &c. Samson exercised his ingenuity in discomfiting the Philistines. But Antichrist will be far more subtle in deluding the faithful. (Menochius) --- The Danites took Lais; afterwards called Cæsarea Philippi, by stratagem, Judges xviii. (Tirinus)

VERSE 19

Gad, being girded, &c. It seems to allude to the tribe of Gad; when, after they had received for their lot the land of Galaad, they marched in arms before the rest of the Israelites, to the conquest of the land of Chanaan: from whence they afterwards returned loaded with spoils. See Josue i. and xxii. (Challoner) --- He alludes continually to the name of Gad, which signifies one "girded, *or* a troop." See Osee vi. 8; Numbers xxxii. 17. (Calmet)

VERSE 20

Fat, delicious. This country was very luxuriant, Deuteronomy xxxiii. 24. (Menochius)

VERSE 21

A hart. Barach was of this tribe, and seemed rather timid, till he was encouraged by Debora; and his victory gave occasion to that beautiful hymn, Judges v. (Calmet)

VERSE 22

Run to and fro, &c. To behold his beauty; whilst his envious brethren turned their darts against him, &c. (Challoner) --- Joseph continued *increasing,* in spite of the envy of his brethren, and the calumny of Putiphar's wife, who was too much enamored of his beauty. (Haydock)

VERSE 24

His bow rested upon the strong, &c. That is, upon God, who was his strength: who also *loosed his bands,* and brought him out of prison to be the *pastor,* that is, the feeder and ruler of Egypt; and the *stone,* that is, the rock and support of Israel.

VERSE 25

Blessings, &c. 1. Of rain; 2. of springs; 3. of milk, (*uberum*); and 4. (*vulvæ*) of children and cattle.

VERSE 26

The blessings of thy father, &c. That is, thy father's blessings are made more prevalent and effectual in thy regard, by the additional strength they receive from his inheriting the blessings of his progenitors Abraham and Isaac. --- *The desire of the everlasting hills,* &c. These blessings all looked forward towards Christ, called *the desire of the everlasting hills,* as being longed for, as it were, by the whole creation. Mystically, the patriarchs and prophets are called the *ever-lasting hills,* by reason of the eminence of their wisdom and holiness. --- *The Nazarite.* This word signifies one *separated;* and agrees to Joseph, as being separated from, and more eminent than, his brethren. As the ancient *Nazarites* were so called from their being set aside for God, and vowed to him. (Challoner) --- *Nazir* denotes also one chosen or *crowned,* and is a title of one of the chief courtiers or ministers of the Persian kings. Such was Joseph. (Calmet) --- These blessings were perhaps forfeited by the misconduct of his posterity, when Jeroboam set up the worship of the golden calves; though probably many would subsist of the tribes of Ephraim and Manasses till the coming of the Messias. (Tirinus)

VERSE 27

Wolf; alluding to the wars in the defense of the inhabitants of Gabaa, and those waged by Saul, Mardocheus, &c. (Menochius) (Judges xix and xx) St. Paul was of this tribe; and, from a fiery zealot, became an eminent apostle. (St. Augustine, &c.) (Tirinus)

VERSE 28

Proper blessings, or predictions; for Ruben received no blessing. (Haydock)

To be gathered to my people. That is, I am going to die, and so to follow my ancestors that are gone before me, and to join their company in another world. (Challoner) --- Jacob's life was embittered with many afflictions, which he bore with admirable patience, and thus deserved to be considered as an excellent figure of Jesus Christ. --- *The man of sorrows.* His faith in the promises of God, made him contemplate the land of Chanaan as his own, and parcel it out among his children. (Calmet)

CHAPTER L
VERSE 1

Kissing him, as it was then the custom, in testimony of an ardent affection. (Menochius)

VERSE 2

Physicians, whose business it was to embalm dead bodies, with a composition of myrrh, &c., in order to keep them from putrefaction, (Menochius) as the Egyptian mummies are treated. (Haydock) --- The entrails are taken out, &c., by the embalmer during 30 days, and the body is left in salt and various drugs, for other 40, in all 70 days, as Herodotus informs us, (B. xi. 86,) and as Moses here insinuates, ver. 3. This was an honor peculiar to the kings. Before any person was buried, his praises were rehearsed; and it was lawful on this occasion to declare, what evil even the kings themselves had done; which sometimes caused them to be deprived of funeral honors. We have several funeral canticles preserved in Scripture: 2 Kings i. 18; iii. 33; 2 Paralipomenon xxxv. 25. (Calmet) --- The Lamentations of Jeremias were perhaps of this nature, on the death of King Josias. The usual time for mourning among the Jews, was 30 days for people of eminence, (Numbers xx; Deuteronomy xxxiv. 8; Procopius) and seven for the rest, Ecclesiasticus xxii. 13. (Haydock)

VERSE 4

Expired. Before the corpse was interred, Joseph could not lay aside his mourning attire, in which it was not lawful to appear at court. (Calmet)

VERSE 5

Dug, in the sepulcher which Abraham had purchased. This circumstance, and the exact words here used by Joseph, are not mentioned elsewhere. (Haydock)

VERSE 7

Ancients; chief officers. (Calmet) --- This is a name of dignity; like our aldermen. (Haydock)

VERSE 10

Atad, which was so called, from being encompassed with *thorns.* (Calmet) --- *Beyond;* with relation to Moses, (Haydock) or on the west side of *the Jordan.* (Calmet)

VERSE 11

Mourning: Hebrew, "Ebel Mitsraim beyond the Jordan." On this occasion they fasted till the evening: perhaps they also cut their flesh and plucked their hair, according to the manners of the Egyptians, which customs (Leviticus xix. 28; Deuteronomy xiv. 1) were prohibited to the Jews. (Tirinus)

VERSE 16

A message; perhaps by Benjamin. (Menochius) --- They hope thus to obtain pardon for the sake of their deceased father, and for the sake of their common God.

VERSE 17

Wept, that they should entertain no doubts respecting the reconciliation, which had taken place seventeen years before. (Haydock)

VERSE 19

Resist, &c. Hebrew, "Am I not subject to God; *or,* Am I a God," to oppose his will. Septuagint, "I belong to the Lord." You see that your designs against me have turned to our mutual advantage. Can I, therefore, think of punishing you? Repent, and obtain pardon of God: I certainly forgive you. (Haydock) --- Thus God drew good out of the evil, in which he had no share. (St. Augustine, City of God xiv. 27; St. Chrysostom, hom. 67.)

VERSE 22

And ten; consequently he had been governor of all the land eighty years; God having made him abundant recompense, even in this world, for a transient disgrace! (Haydock) ---

Knees. Joseph adopted the only son of Machir. See chap. xxx. 3; or, according to the Samaritan, "in the days of Joseph" he was born. (Calmet)

VERSE 24

Visit you with various persecutions; or will fulfill his promises. --- *Carry my bones.* He would have them to keep his bones till the time of their departure, as an earnest that they should certainly obtain the land of Chanaan; and thus his *bones were visited, and after death, they prophesied,* Ecclesiasticus xlix. 18. Perhaps the Egyptians would have been offended, (Worthington) if the corpse of Joseph had been removed out of the country immediately, as that of Jacob was; and they might have taken occasion hence to envy and persecute his brethren. (Haydock)

VERSE 25

Embalmed, like the Egyptian momies, or *mummies,* which is a Persian word, signifying a dried corpse. Some of them are very magnificent, adorned with golden letters and hieroglyphics, various bandages, &c. They are laid in coffins. Some pretend that Joseph was afterwards adored in Egypt, under the names of Serapis and Osiris: but the grounds of this supposition are only a few uncertain etymologies and emblems, which might agree with him as well as with those modern deities: (Calmet) at least it does not at all appear probable, that he was adored in Egypt before the departure of the Israelites, as the king who persecuted them did not know Joseph, Exodus i. 8. His greatest glory was, to have prefigured Jesus Christ in so wonderful a manner during the course of his life, and to have been replenished with all the graces which could form the character of a great man and a saint. Some think, that the history of Joseph has been imitated in the fable of Proteus, or Cetes, king of Egypt. See the True History of Fabulous Times, by Juerin du Roche, a virtuous and learned ecclesiastic, who we put to death for his faith, at Paris, September 8, 1792. See also Rollin's Abridgment. (Haydock)

CPSIA information can be obtained
at www.ICGtesting.com
Printed in the USA
LVHW080229120321
681333LV00015B/336